AIR UNIVERSITY

AIR FORCE RESEARCH INSTITUTE

Learning to Leave

The Preeminence of Disengagement in US Military Strategy

R. GREG BROWN
Major, USAF

Drew Paper No. 3

Air University Press
Maxwell Air Force Base, Alabama 36112-5962

May 2008

Muir S. Fairchild Research Information Center Cataloging Data

Brown, R. Greg.
    Learning to leave : the preeminence of disengagement in US military strategy /
R. Greg Brown.
        p. ; cm. – (Drew paper, 1941-3785 ; no. 3)
    Includes bibliographical references.
    ISBN 978-1-58566-181-7.
    1. Strategy. 2. Disengagement (Military science) 3. War—Termination. 4. United
States—Military policy. I. Title. II. Series.

    355.02—dc22

Disclaimer

This Drew Paper and others in the series are available electronically at the Air University Research Web site http://research.maxwell.af.mil and the AU Press Web site http://aupress.maxwell.af.mil.

The Drew Papers

The Drew Papers are occasional publications sponsored by the Air Force Research Institute (AFRI), Maxwell AFB, Alabama. AFRI publishes this series of papers to commemorate the distinguished career of Col Dennis "Denny" Drew, USAF, retired. In 30 years at Air University, Colonel Drew served on the Air Command and Staff College faculty, directed the Airpower Research Institute, and served as dean, associate dean, and professor of military strategy at the School of Advanced Air and Space Studies, Maxwell AFB. Colonel Drew is one of the Air Force's most extensively published authors and an international speaker in high demand. He has lectured to over 100,000 students at Air University as well as to foreign military audiences. In 1985 he received the Muir S. Fairchild Award for outstanding contributions to Air University. In 2003 Queen Beatrix of the Netherlands made him a Knight in the Order of Orange-Nassau for his contributions to education in the Royal Netherlands Air Force.

The Drew Papers are dedicated to promoting the understanding of air and space power theory and application. These studies are published by the Air University Press and broadly distributed throughout the US Air Force, the Department of Defense, and other governmental organizations, as well as to leading scholars, selected institutions of higher learning, public-policy institutes, and the media.

All military members and civilian employees assigned to Air University are invited to contribute unclassified manuscripts that deal with air and/or space power history, theory, doctrine, or strategy, or with joint or combined service matters bearing on the application of air and/or space power.

Authors should submit three copies of a double-spaced, typed manuscript and an electronic version of the manuscript on removable media along with a brief (200-word maximum) abstract. The electronic file should be compatible with Microsoft Windows and Microsoft Word—Air University Press uses Word as its standard word-processing program.

Please send inquiries or comments to
Director
Air Force Research Institute
155 N. Twining St.
Maxwell AFB, AL 36112-6026
Tel: (334) 953-9587
DSN 493-9587
Fax: (334) 953-6739
DSN 493-6739
E-mail: research.support@maxwell.af.mil

Contents

Illustrations

CONTENTS

Tables

Foreword

National security strategy (NSS) changes from president to president. These changes are often referred to as doctrines. Some represent explicit grand strategy, while others require examinations of policy to ferret out. Their enduring traits, however, are most important to national military strategy (NMS). What has endured in America's superpower experience since World War II is that the United States engages forward in times of peace and fights forward in times of war.

In this respect, Maj R. Greg Brown's *Learning to Leave* informs strategy at the highest stations of power. He notes that strategy is about managing context and that the context of US national security changed with the end of the Cold War, although its organizing framework did not fundamentally change. Through a thoughtful synthesis of history and organizational theory, Major Brown reveals misperceptions that add to the outdated security framework to further hinder disengagement. In the nexus of the end of the Cold War, the peace dividend, and an increasingly expansive NSS, he finds the historical parallel between the NSS and the NMS no longer appropriate, as it leads military and civilian policy makers to overextend the military.

The rather counterintuitive conclusion that follows is that to sustain an expansive NSS of engagement, conflicts—when they arise—must be planned with an eye on disengagement of military forces at the earliest reasonable opportunity. As strategic military disengagement is anathema to our national security apparatus and military culture, it must demand preeminence in the NMS to ensure timely disengagement.

Regarding current conflicts, Major Brown avoids prescriptions. As we approach the historical inflection point between presidential doctrines, however, we have an opportunity to consider if the end of the Cold War, progress in the current struggle against violent extremism, or the global strategic environment of the twenty-first century warrants a reassessment of our national security structures and policies and the relationship between NSS and NMS.

Major Brown writes with a command of the facts and a compelling style. This work is in various degrees historical, theoretical, counterintuitive, and shocking. While certainly not an airpower treatise, it offers keen observations and sound lessons on the use of the proper force for the objective, and it resonates with the inherent advantages that airpower provides national security decision makers. Originally written as a master's thesis for Air University's School of Advanced Air and Space Studies (SAASS), *Learning to Leave* was selected by the Air University Foundation as the best SAASS thesis for academic year 2006–7. It is a fitting installment for the Drew Papers. I am pleased to commend this excellent study and am encouraged by what it portends for national security thought in the ranks of our Air Force.

DAVID A. DEPTULA, Lt Gen, USAF
Deputy Chief of Staff, Intelligence,
Surveillance, and Reconnaissance

About the Author

Maj R. Greg Brown was commissioned through the United States Air Force Reserve Officer Training Corps in 1992 as a distinguished graduate. He received a bachelor's degree in Russian Studies from the University of Oklahoma. After graduating from Intelligence Technical Training in 1993, he served as the first-ever chief of intelligence for the B-1B Formal Training Unit. He subsequently attended the Air Force Weapons School, followed by service as an intelligence weapons officer for a composite wing and the provisional wing supporting Operation Southern Watch. While assigned as an instructor at the Air Force Weapons School, he obtained a master's degree in Aeronautical Science from Embry-Riddle Aeronautical University. He deployed as the intelligence duty officer in the combined air operations center during Operation Enduring Freedom. Major Brown then served on the Air Staff as action officer and program element monitor for a portfolio of intelligence, surveillance, and reconnaissance infrastructure programs in excess of $2 billion, all focused on operational- and tactical-level unit support.

In the immediate aftermath of Operation Iraqi Freedom major combat operations, Major Brown again deployed to the combined air operations center, this time as the Air Force forces deputy director for intelligence. He was then selected to be the director of operations for the 609th Air Intelligence Squadron and was directly responsible for all intelligence operations in the Central Command Air Forces area of operations. In 2006 Major Brown graduated from the Air Force Institute of Technology Intermediate Developmental Education program with a master's degree in Strategic Leadership and immediately entered the School of Advanced Air and Space Studies. Major Brown, his wife Laura, and twin boys Payton and Blake, left Maxwell for Washington, DC, and a second Air Staff tour.

Editor's Note: Major Brown was promoted to lieutenant colonel effective 1 April 2008 and subsequently selected to command the 547th Intelligence Squadron at Nellis AFB, Nevada.

Acknowledgments

The initial idea for this thesis came from a study that Dr. Richard Andres and others at Air University worked for the chief of staff of the Air Force, Gen T. Michael Moseley. The study explored ways the US Air Force could use airpower to help US ground forces disengage from operations in Iraq. Intrigued by the question and skeptical of popularly espoused analogies to Vietnam, I nonetheless latched on to the idea of there being fundamental lessons from past wars that the United States fails to learn. From this experience came the title, *Learning to Leave,* and a rough outline of how airpower could help land forces to disengage.

From there, thanks go to Dr. Everett Dolman, who, upon reading the proposal, told me he liked nothing about it, except the title. Convinced the prevailing efforts to find "how" to disengage missed a larger point, Dr. Dolman was "smitten" with the idea of learning to disengage, believing it went well beyond popular notions and could seriously expand on some points intimated but never made by Clausewitz. While this thesis does not pretend to fill gaps found in *On War*, it is hard to walk away from "smitten."

Thanks for the evolution go to Dr. Stephen Chiabotti, my primary thesis advisor and always a thoughtful backboard off which I could bounce ideas. His suggestion of excessive congruence between national security strategy and national military strategy established a central theme to this thesis. Despite a busy schedule and experiencing a personal tragedy, Dr. Chiabotti helped me to navigate through the process, questioned my ideas, offered alternative approaches, and thoroughly read multiple drafts.

Finally, but foremost, love, thanks, and great gratitude go to my wife, Laura. Her patience made this immeasurably easier. Over the months of evening reading and typing, she never complained about her "half-husband" or home but rarely really "disengaged" from work. This, on top of five moves in as many years, with preschoolers and a business in tow, and yet never a negative word. I am blessed.

Chapter 1

Introduction
Disengagement in Context

In this report, we make a number of recommendations for actions to be taken in Iraq, the United States, and the region. Our most important recommendations call for new and enhanced diplomatic and political efforts in Iraq and the region and a change in the primary mission of US forces in Iraq that will enable the United States to begin to move its combat forces out of Iraq responsibly. We believe that these two recommendations are equally important and reinforce one another.

—Iraq Study Group Report
6 December 2006

Continuation is the goal of strategy—not culmination.

—Everett Dolman, *Pure Strategy*

One can no more achieve final victory than one can "win" history.

—Christopher Bassford
"John Keegan and the Tradition
of Trashing Clausewitz"

Even before the release of the *Iraq Study Group Report*, a storm was brewing over how and when United States (US) forces should withdraw from Iraq. The debate is not new. The storm started building when it became clear that the fall of Saddam Hussein would not resolve the Iraq issue. As the insurgency gained steam, US media began asking about exit strategies. As sectarian violence became more widespread, political figures such as Rep. Jack Murtha began calling for withdrawal of US forces. Others, including Senator Joe Biden and Council on Foreign Relations president emeritus Dr. Leslie Gelb have proposed dividing Iraq along sectarian lines to help facilitate a quick US withdrawal.[1] The building impatience among the US populace with the lack of withdrawal of US forces was partly responsible for the party shift in the November 2006 midterm congressional elections. This study suggests the problems of disengagement have deeper roots than the start of the insurgency in Iraq.

Disengagement on the National Agenda

Some in the administration of Pres. George W. Bush questioned the war plan in the buildup to the 2003 invasion.[2] There was a conspicuous lack of planning for post-combat operations, referred to by military planners as phase IV, or commonly called the exit strategy. The idea of having an exit strategy before undertaking a military operation harkens back to the Vietnam War and reflects what has come to be known as the Powell Doctrine.[3] Many critics of President Bush's Iraq strategy use the lack of a clear exit strategy to draw analogies between the quagmire in Iraq and America's Vietnam experience. While valid parallels abound between the two conflicts, the Vietnam analogy is too simplistic to inform policy; instead, *quagmire* serves mainly as a political pejorative.[4] This study looks beyond simplistic pejoratives and delusional how-to prescriptions in the hopes of making a case for why disengagement supports an effective grand strategy.

Advancing the Ball

A larger and more serious problem is overlooked while policy makers and pundits argue over *how* to disengage from Iraq. No one seems to be asking *why* the US military repeatedly finds itself in this spot. This paper examines the tendency for the US military to remain engaged in regions well after victory occurs. Moreover, it explores the use of the military instrument of national power in situations not including combat operations. Ultimately, this study seeks to answer the question Does the congruence in language between national security strategy (NSS) and national military strategy (NMS) actually discourage disengagement, by misaligning means to ends, as national security strategy becomes more expansive?

Propositions

Far from dealing with problems unique to Iraq—or even simply analogous to Vietnam—this study posits a systemic flaw in the translation of grand strategy in the form of NSS into NMS. It examines the following four propositions:

1. The disengagement of military forces, like their engagement, is a decision made by the president, consistent with the NSS, and executed through the NMS. The NMS must be conducive to disengagement.

2. The decision to disengage is part of strategy making, a fundamentally joint, interagency, organizational phenomenon. As a strategy-making organization, the US national security apparatus erects barriers to disengagement, as it is outdated—still reflecting a Cold War framework—and flawed and biased toward the engagement of military forces.

3. Inappropriate congruence between NMS and NSS discourages disengagement and invites quagmires, particularly as expansive NSS encourages greater use of the military to a lower standard of national interests. Expansive US national security strategies thus tend to overextend the military's capabilities.

4. Engagement is critically flawed as an NMS because it causes misperceptions of (a) the use of military force as being the end of a linear progression of policy options, thus making military disengagement a retreat, (b) victory (battle) as synonymous with resolution (policy), (c) the lack of necessity to plan for disengagement, and (d) military engagement in major combat operations necessarily requiring military presence in post-combat operations.

Background and Significance of the Problem

The debate over *how* to get out of Iraq is a contemporary iteration of a historical theme. The question of *how* is a valid and difficult question of mechanics, but preventing the situation is preferred to continually reacting to similar situations. As a na-

3

tion, America finds itself in this quandary because of larger policy decisions. In the decades since World War II, the United States has operated under national security strategies of increased international involvement. In the bipolar power environment of the Cold War, containment involved encouraging nations into the Western sphere while discouraging their relations with the Eastern bloc. After the Soviet Union fell, the subsequent national security strategies evolved to "engagement and enlargement."[5] As an unintended consequence and as US national military strategies have mirrored the NSS, various barriers to disengaging military forces have emerged. America must recognize that this phenomenon limits US national policy options. By consciously considering the need for disengagement in US military strategic calculus, the nation preserves the policy potential of military force.

Today's question, How do we disengage in Iraq? is an issue because the United States fails to distinguish between engagement in military terms and the other elements of national power: diplomacy, information, and economics. This phenomenon is rooted in America's more than 50-year presence in Germany, Japan, and Korea. Every troop left in place is a troop unavailable for his or her primary mission—combat. If the United States cannot strategically manage disengagement, the United States removes the potential for a military extension of our national policy in Iran, North Korea, and elsewhere.

Methodology

This study follows a systematic approach, positing propositions, offering support, and consolidating lessons for future policy makers. Theoretical underpinnings of disengagement are laid out, and then post–World War II military interventions are examined as minicases. Primary sources consist of such policy documents as the NSS and NMS reports. Secondary sources include written accounts of recent wars.

Literature Review

This study fills a gap in existing literature. Theories on war, victory, and political power seem to overlook military disengagement as a critical process—or they assume it away. In his seminal work, *On War*, Carl von Clausewitz focused on the root cause of war as a political tool and on the conduct of war. He wrote around disengagement in one of his more oft-quoted lines: "No one starts a war—or rather, no one in his senses ought to do so—without first being clear in his mind what he intends to achieve by that war and how he intends to conduct it."[6] This hints at the need for aligning the military means with the policy end in mind. Here, he distinguished between tactical and strategic ends and means: "In tactics the means are the fighting forces . . . the end is victory."[7] In the broader view of strategy, this tactical end of victory becomes "the original means of strategy" and "its ends . . . are those objects which will lead directly to peace."[8] B. H. Liddell Hart expressed this strategic "object of war" more clearly as "a better state of peace."[9]

In a tactical sense, it is enough, as Clausewitz said, "that the enemy's withdrawal from the battlefield is the sign of *victory*."[10] Unfortunately, *victory* is a term that begs for use at the strategic level as well. Most of the war literature throws around the term *victory* indiscriminately. Thus, in the modern context, defining *victory* is a major obstacle in strategy. Robert Mandel tackles this definition in *The Meaning of Military Victory*, claiming that "perhaps the least understood, and certainly the least studied, aspect of wars is how they end. . . . The most difficult problem caused by contemporary warfare, all in all, is the difficulty of achieving a stable, secure ending to it."[11]

H. E. Goemans, in *War and Punishment*, agrees with Mandel, saying, "While it is interesting and important to know why wars break out in the first place, it is no less interesting or important to know why it often takes so much time and such enormous costs before wars end."[12] In Goemans's view, the fundamental cause of war termination is a change in the minimum terms of settlement of the combatants. Goemans shows that some regimes refuse to lower their war aims, and, in fact, raise them "*even when they learn they will probably lose*" (emphasis in original).[13] His central proposition is "that the decision to continue fighting or settle depends on the nature of the domestic political regime."[14] Such semirepressive, moderately exclusionary regimes as Slobodan Milosevic's Serbia refuse to lower their war aims and prefer to continue fighting because they expect severe domestic punishment for even a moderate defeat. Repressive, exclusionary regimes, including Saddam Hussein's Iraq, tend to gamble often, as there is little risk of internal consequence for failed policies or moderate defeats, but they settle quickly if defeat appears catastrophic, as there is no existential threat to the regime for moderate defeats. In the final case, nonrepressive, nonexclusionary regimes, like Western democracies, prefer to lower their aims to end conflict.[15]

Goemans's final case, along with the inherent subjectivity of victory, is doubly problematic for contemporary American warfare. America does not want to be seen as benefiting materially from interventions for fear of being perceived as imperialistic. G. John Ikenberry addresses this and other issues in the aftermath of major wars in *After Victory*. His central question is What do states that have just won major wars do with their newly acquired power? Ikenberry concludes that states "have sought to hold on to that power and make it last, and that this has led these states, paradoxically, to find ways to set limits on their power and make it acceptable to other states."[16]

Ikenberry's thesis points to an institutional mismatch as complicating the defining of victory and determining how and when to disengage military forces. Thomas Barnett touches on this organizational dilemma in *The Pentagon's New Map* and points to the need for what he terms a system administrator force to specialize in post-conflict operations.[17]

In the United States, grand strategy coincides with what is commonly referred to as a president's doctrine. Massachusetts Institute of Technology political science scholar Barry Posen sees grand strategy, or national security strategy, as "a political-military means-ends chain."[18] In *The Sources of Military Doctrine*, Posen beleives that organizational theory provides a good explanation for the operational preferences and behavior of military organizations. Whereas Posen argues that the balance-of-power theory better explains the character of doctrine, this study explores organizational dysfunction in the national security apparatus. In general, Posen finds that organizational theory predicts offensive, disintegrated, and military doctrines, as organizational factors tend to work against integrated grand strategies.[19] Organization theory predicts that militaries frequently will behave in ways that are inimical to the interests of the state.[20]

Disengagement decisions often are in the interest of the state but too often are set aside. Framing, a branch of organizational theory, offers a much more comprehensive means by which to analyze a complex organization like the Department of Defense or moreover, the national security apparatus. Organizational theorists Lee Bolman and Terrence Deal show the explanatory strengths and weaknesses of the framework—to include its internal consistency, comprehensiveness, and external validity—in their seminal work, *Reframing Organizations*.[21] Framing is a useful tool both for explaining past events and for predicting future ones and thus should help shed light on barriers that prevent strategic military disengagement.

On the military side, there are mountains of documents outlining tactical lessons learned from military operations. Standard operating procedures, tactics, and a variety of manuals and regulations have sprung from these reports. Similarly, at the operational level, tiger teams put together similar lessons-learned documents. Their prescriptions add to the wealth of historical experience in the form of doctrine. A gap seems to exist at the national military-strategic level to ensure the NMS is appropriate for the capabilities and limitations of the military force.

Thesis Statement

This study determines why the United States has trouble disengaging military forces at the appropriate time. Put another way, if war is a continuation of policy by other means, when military victory occurs, disengaging the military follows as continuing the national policy by less violent means. Victory is the desired end in battle. A better state of peace is the desired end in war. Continuing advantage is the desired end of strategy. The timely disengagement of military forces preserves maximum potential for the military instrument of policy; therefore, disengagement is the best NMS in support of expansive NSS.

Preview of Arguments

Chapter 2 defines strategic military disengagement in the historical context of the so-called Western way of war. Disengagement thus resides within the concepts of war initiation, historical means of war fighting, the concept of victory, and war resolution. The chapter further explains how the NMS flows from the NSS and examines how congruence develops between the two.

Chapters 3 and 4 consider how US national security strategy influences strategic military disengagement decisions. More specifically, they examine the supposed necessary congruence between NSS and its subordinate NMS. An outline of historical national security strategies since World War II relates to concurrent national military strategies. Relevant conflicts of the periods are used as the lens to examine the congruence and appropriateness of the NMS to NSS. Chapter 3 covers the Cold War period, while chapter 4 examines the post–Cold War New World Order.

Chapter 5 takes the evidence from chapters 3 and 4 and searches for forces that prevent decision makers from considering, or at least choosing, disengagement. Recognized flaws in the US national security apparatus, which ultimately led to the Goldwater-Nichols Department of Defense Reorganization Act, are used to frame the issue of disengagement in organizational terms less obvious—but ultimately more enlightening—than those typical of bureaucratic reform panels and commissions. The chapter posits barriers to disengagement in the US national security apparatus to determine if such weaknesses prevent correctly linking the national security strategy to the national military strategy.

Chapter 6 explores two macro-level results of the barriers to disengagement that exist in the US national security apparatus. The chapter first lays out common cultural misperceptions in concepts and terminology that tend to make disengagement difficult. It then posits several perceptions of strategy generally and military force that cause disengagement to be seen negatively. The chapter also shows how an overly optimistic, excessively ideological NSS can lead to an NMS that, to maintain congruency, overextends the capabilities, roles, and missions of the armed forces as an element of national power.

Chapter 7, "Conclusion," summarizes key findings. This study avoids prescriptions but proposes implications for disengagement in the future.

Notes

(Notes for this chapter and the following chapters appear in shortened form. For full details, see appropriate entries in the bibliography.)

1. Biden, Jr., "A Plan to Hold Iraq Together."
2. Gordon and Trainor, *Cobra II*, 149.
3. Often erroneously called the Weinberger Doctrine. Colin Powell, who had learned the lessons of Vietnam firsthand, was Secretary of Defense Caspar Weinberger's military assistant. Powell added the explicit call for an exit strategy to Weinberger's tests for commitment of US military forces.
4. Record, *Comparing Iraq and Vietnam*. Dr. Jeffrey Record points out the parallels and significant differences between the conflicts in Iraq and Vietnam, warning of dangers inherent in analogies. For a more extensive argument, see Record, *Dark Victory*.
5. Clinton, *A National Security Strategy of Engagement and Enlargement*.
6. Clausewitz, *On War*, 579.
7. Ibid., 142.
8. Ibid., 143.
9. Liddell Hart, *Strategy*, 338.
10. Clausewitz, *On War*, 142.
11. Mandel, *The Meaning of Military Victory*, 2. See also Alvert and Luck, eds., *On the Endings of Wars*, 3; and Johnson, *Morality and Contemporary Warfare*, 191.
12. Goemans, *War and Punishment*, 3.
13. Ibid., 4.
14. Ibid.
15. Ibid.
16. Ikenberry, *After Victory*, xi.
17. Barnett, *The Pentagon's New Map*.
18. Posen, *The Sources of Military Doctrine*, 220.
19. Ibid., 222–39.
20. Ibid., 241.
21. Bolman and Deal, *Reframing Organizations*.

Chapter 2

Disengagement in Strategy
The Western Way of War

You can disengage from a friend or ally by unilateral action. Disengagement from an enemy requires bilateral action.

—Hans Speier
Disengagement

(The contemporary American Way of War seeks) . . . a quick victory with minimal casualties on both sides. Its hallmarks are speed, maneuver, flexibility, and surprise. It is heavily reliant on precision firepower, special forces, and psychological operations.

—Max Boot
"The New American Way of War"

This chapter defines *strategic military disengagement* in the historical context of the so-called Western way of war. Disengagement is enveloped in the concepts of war initiation, historical means of war fighting, the concept of victory, and war resolution. The chapter further explains how the NMS flows from the NSS and examines how congruence develops between the two.

Disengagement

The first requirement for discussing *disengagement* is to define disengagement. The term, as used in this study, is virtually nonexistent in the strategic literature. Joint doctrine defines *disengagement* as "in arms control, a general term for proposals that would result in the geographic separation of opposing non-indigenous forces without directly affecting indigenous military forces."[1] While the concept is applicable, as removal of US (non-indigenous) forces is the intent, the arms control caveat distorts the term. The term appears in other doctrine publications but usually to denote a more tactical connotation of withdrawal of forces from battle "to break off a military action with an enemy."[2] In terms of "release from an engagement, pledge, or obligation," the author believes *disengagement* is an overlooked or underappreciated phase of conflict that is tied up somewhere in the ambiguity of victory and war termination.[3] Its importance in terms of national security strategy is apparent in the US history of being bogged down in unforeseen long-term engagements.

The joint definition of *disengagement* reflects the historical strategic literature, where disengagement appears predominantly in Cold War proposals for redeployment of US forces, primarily from Europe. Contemporary usage is focused on such counterinsurgency operations as Israeli disengagement from Palestinian territories and US disengagement from Iraq. The historic nuclear and the contemporary counterinsurgency contexts allude to the concept of disengagement discussed in this study, but they are not complete. Theoretical literature on the concept of strategic military disengagement is lacking.

The existing literature offers a valuable baseline from which to start discussing disengagement. Foremost among the sources surveyed is a 1958 RAND study that defines the following important tenets of disengagement:

1. Disengagement from an enemy requires bilateral action.
2. Disengagement can be forced if the enemy lacks a credible threat.
3. Disengagement decisions can be based on present and future intentions.[4]

Written in the nuclear context, the base tenets apply equally to conventional and irregular conflicts. The unstated assumption is the understanding that one always can disengage, provided one does not object to the cost. Given that, the first tenet of disengagement is RAND analyst Hans Speier's quote that opened this chapter. Speier illustrates his point in post–World War II Europe, where the United States could have redeployed its forces to the United States without the consent of the United Kingdom, France, or other Allies. The Allies tried to block such action with joint security arrangements. Disengaging from the Soviet Union, on the other hand, required assurances from the Soviet Union that it would not capitalize on the resulting shift in the balance of power in Europe. Following this tenet of disengagement, the United States could have disengaged unilaterally from the Korean peninsula in 1953, but disengagement required assurances from the North or its sponsors. The same applied in Vietnam and applies today in Iraq. The United States can leave Iraq with no actions required of the Iraqi national government but not without assurances from the antigovernment forces.

If the first tenet essentially asserts the old saw of war that the enemy gets a vote, then the second tenet points out a caveat. The enemy's vote only counts if it carries weight. Disengagement can be forced if the enemy lacks the strength to pose a credible threat to national interests. For example, the United States needs assurances from antigovernment forces in Iraq because they pose a credible threat. The same was true of the Soviets in Europe and the North Koreans. It was also true of the Vietcong and the North Vietnamese Army for nearly a decade. The Vietnam case illustrates that the threat in absolute terms is not what matters, but what matters is its weight against US national interests. By 1972, US interests had shifted to the point that the same threat from North Vietnam that warranted US engagement in 1965 was no longer sufficiently important to US interests to warrant remaining engaged.

The Taliban and al-Qaeda in Afghanistan represent these first two tenets. The Taliban lost the strength to maintain government control in December 2001 and effectively surrendered all territories. Al-Qaeda lost its safe haven. Yet, the United States could not disengage from the global war on terror. The Taliban are dissatisfied and out of power, and the terrorists continue to pose a threat. Thwarting al-Qaeda in Afghanistan does not preclude meeting them again in Iraq, Europe, or elsewhere.

Speier's third tenet states that disengagement decisions can be based on estimates of present and future intentions. Of particular interest in limited conflicts where military force is less able to produce decisive victory, this tenet means military disengagement may be appropriate if military power is not the primary element of national power targeted by the enemy. George Kennan's criticism from the 1950s of the "over-militarization of thinking in the West" is still argued today and points to this condition for disengagement.[5] In its simplest form, the third tenet hints that with the military instrument of power removed from the calculus, diplomatic and economic means may be reasonable if the enemy is viewed as liable to abandon aggressive intentions in exchange for an acceptable concession. Negotiations can be requested when escalation is the driving concern.

Common to the 1958 Cold War nuclear environment and today's Israel/Palestine or US/Iraq situations is one ultimate question: Are the results of disengagement likely to be worse than the current policy and if so, are they irreversible? Can we afford disengagement "if there is any chance it's wrong or may become wrong based on disengagement?"[6] Leaders must answer this question in terms of national security strategy. *A strategy emphasizing military disengagement, whenever reasonable, leaves more credible military threats on the table for follow-on crises.* (emphasis added) While easy to say, disengagement does not just happen. It must be planned as diligently as major combat operations are planned. In the terms of the Powell Doctrine, "Have a clear political objective and stick to it. Use all the force necessary, and do not apologize for going in big if that is what it takes. Decisive force ends wars quickly and in the long run saves lives."[7] The implication is that lives are saved by winning quickly and exiting in accordance with the strategy vice going in with open-ended objectives.

Speier notes the importance of disengagement decisions remaining in the realm of sound national policy instead of relying on public or international opinion. "It is the fate of great powers to be criticized by lesser powers and it is salutary in democracy to voice political misgivings," says Speier, "but foreign policy cannot be conducted as though it were a national or international popularity contest."[8] Caspar W. Weinberger and Colin Powell conflict with Speier in their call for reasonable assurance of public support before engaging US forces. It is the nature of democracies that the people's voices eventually will win out. Public opinion in the United States favors disengagement. The very essence of *quagmire* in the United States is the erosion of public support in the face of prolonged interventions with seemingly unimportant or unattainable objectives.

One final note remains on what disengagement is not before the discussion continues with what it is. A key misconception of disengagement assumes that it is complete. While it is possible to disengage completely in all areas of national power, this study posits military disengagement as a means of allowing more room for other elements of national power to operate, while at the same time freeing the military instrument for future needs. While Speier defined some tenets of disengagement nearly 50 years ago, contemporary literature deals with it only obliquely, tied up somewhere in the discussions of victory and war termination. Often disengagement is swathed in equally nebulous terms like *end state*, *termination criteria*, and *exit strategy*.

Determinants of Disengagement

Clausewitz famously entreated leaders to know what kind of war they are fighting before engaging in it. Not surprisingly, the vast majority of the literature on warfare deals with why wars start and how they are conducted. Countless schools of thought abound on these subjects, each with its own typology. Noted British historian and president emeritus of the International Institute for Strategic Studies, Sir Michael Howard, provided a concise history of European warfare that serves as a jumping-off point for the study of American warfare. Howard tracks European war from fifth-century-BC Greece up to the Cold War, combining political science, sociological, economic, and demographic theories.[9] Irrespective of the theoretical base, however, it seems logical that the type of war also affects the means of disengaging forces.

Victory

However wars start and regardless of how they are fought, each side has a desired end in mind. This end is generically labeled victory. Victory, whatever end state it may represent, is a desirable precondition for disengagement to occur. The literature on war is rich with assertions like Gen Douglas MacArthur's that "in war there is no substitute for victory."[10] Despite the term's wide use, little agreement exists on what makes for victory, especially at the strategic level. While MacArthur was right about its use at the tactical level, in strategic terms "military victory . . . is neither necessary nor sufficient for people to think a leader has won."[11] It is possible to be seen as victorious despite losses along the way, as would be the argument for the North Vietnamese victory over the United States. Likewise, tactical victory is not sufficient, as evidenced by the argument that

15

the United States won the battles in Vietnam but didn't achieve perceived victory. Therefore, it is fair to say that "victory in war is much larger and more dearly obtained than success in military operations."[12]

Most of the literature on victory's place in war examines specific conflicts, reconstruction techniques, and nation building. Robert Mandel identifies state-level deficiencies in the West and system-level deficiencies in the global "rules of the game" that impede achievement of meaningful victory. He identifies specific conditions under which strategic victory is likely to follow military victory and details the trade-offs between morality and stability that achieving strategic victory may entail.[13] One of the problems with defining victory is that the desired political end state is usually identified in ambiguous terms.

The concept of victory is intrinsically tied to any concept of war. Clausewitz claims that no one should engage in war without first knowing what to gain. Liddell Hart asserts that the desired end should be a better state of peace. From this it follows that "the first aim in war is to win, the second is to prevent defeat, the third is to shorten it, and the fourth and the most important, which must never be lost to sight, is to make a just and durable peace."[14]

Termination and a Better State of Peace

Whether or not war leads to a better state of peace in political and economic terms generally depends on the aims going in and the scope of the engagement. Wars with limited aims and low stakes might end in stalemate, when loss of life and property are seen to outweigh potential gains. Suits for peace may result in treaties that resolve territorial and other claims. When a warring party surrenders, it may do so conditionally if the victor will negotiate. Alternatively, the victor may dictate terms the vanquished must accept to prevent further harm to life and property.

Two things are true in war termination. First, the linkage to disengagement is seen in the fact that termination is dependent always on agreement between the parties. Wars terminate in only a handful of generic ways. As the reasons for—and means of—fighting wars has varied throughout history, and so have the means of war termination. The least complicated and yet likely the harshest means is by capitulation, where one party unilaterally recognizes its inability to continue military action. This is the basis of unconditional surrender, and in its extreme form, it can include annihilation of the vanquished. When intentions are less severe and a consensus can be reached, peace treaties typically leap to mind as the classic means. By one count, however, only 137 of the 311 wars that took place from 1480 to 1970 ended with a formal treaty. Other means include a cease-fire and an armistice; the former connoting a stop to hostilities and the latter being a temporary cessation of hostilities to facilitate negotiations.[15] Regardless of the manner in which a war ends, the vanquished adversary always has a vote. An invader can leave after plundering only if the vanquished state chooses not to continue to fight. Annexation must be accepted by the population, if the invader wishes to disengage military forces. Willingness to exterminate the population is the case that nullifies the others.

According to G. John Ikenberry, the second truism of war termination holds that "states rarely finish wars for the same reasons they start them."[16] This is a particularly poignant point in America's current situation in Iraq. Once a decision to invade is made, bargaining begins toward acceptable terms for ending hostilities.

How the factions finish wars is at least partly determined by the desired *better state of peace* of the victor. Disengagement decisions are affected by how the victor goes about implementing that state of peace after victory. Ikenberry examines this point in his aptly titled *After Victory*. He believes victors generally follow one of three paths in exercising the power that victory bestows on them. The first path is domination, where the victor controls all decisions relative to postwar conflicts. The second, abandonment, occurs once the enemy is vanquished and the victor takes no interest in the postwar situation and returns home. The third, the most complicated, is transformation. In this case, the victor tries to establish a durable state of peace among all the players. This delicate middle ground requires "convincing the weaker/defeated states it will not pursue the other two options."[17] The Peace of Westphalia, which ended the Thirty Years' War in 1648, was an early effort at transformation. The peace focused on the separation and dispersion of state and clerical power to prevent future wars.[18] Such transformational approaches to the better state of peace matured and set the stage for the emergence of the United States as a world power after World War II.

The post–World War II security climate led shortly into the Cold War. The ominous specter of this new form of total global war, nuclear war, limited conflict. As in earlier centuries, this form of engagement was costly. Instead, European powers faced conventional revolutionary wars in their colonies.[19] Longstanding military conflicts are now played out in the context of nuclear deterrence and the superpower ideological standoff. America attempted to transform its new superpower status into a lasting peaceful order in Europe. America tried to lock others into institutions while leaving itself unencumbered. Institutions like the United Nations (UN) and the North Atlantic Treaty Organization eventually limited US exercise of its hegemonic powers. The United States risked unwanted entanglement, and the weaker powers risked domination.[20]

Where historically US forces would disengage and demobilize after foreign expeditions, there appeared a need to maintain a forward military presence to deter the spread of global communism. Traditional roles of US military forces abroad changed as continuous presence led to military forces taking on roles beyond combat. Incongruence developed between the NSS end of nuclear deterrence and the military means. Presence led to the military instrument being used for diplomatic, economic, and informational ends.

By contrast, post–Cold War America apparently faced minor threats, not existential ones like the nationalist ideologies that led to the world wars and the Cold War. Though the world lacked a monolithic, unifying threat, affairs remained chaotic. The US military—along with other Western nations and often under the auspices of the UN—became increasingly occupied with military operations other than war. Such limited liability operations emerged as the standard for acceptable superpower conflict under the Cold War construct. With *peace dividend* budgets, the military had incentives to take on "anything from delivering babies to delivering nuclear weapons."[21] Table 1 shows the congruence in national strategy.

Table 1. Congruence in national strategy

National Security Strategy	National Military Strategy	Congruence	Effectiveness
Pre–WW II Isolationism	Garrison	High	High
Cold-War Communist Containment	Deterrence Forward Presence	High	Mixed
New World Order Engagement	Engagement Expeditionary	High	Low

Source: Author's original conceptualization in discussion with Dr. Stephen Chiabotti, SAASS, February 2007.

The Strategy Hierarchy

History positions disengagement conceptually in the discussion of the Western way of war. By the end of World War II, the Western way had arguably morphed into the American way of war. The US government's view of national security was forever changed by its emergent superpower role. Drastic changes were made to the national security apparatus in the aftermath of World War II to include the establishment of the National Security Council (NSC), the Department of Defense (DOD) over the Army, Navy, and newly created Air Force; and the creation of the nation's first permanent national intelligence community.[22]

The president defines the country's *grand strategy*. This NSS identifies the nation's foreign policy interests and the threats posed to them and outlines how the president aims to deal with those threats. The strategy indicates the president's preferred balance of the instruments of national power—diplomatic, information, military, and economic.

The DOD issues a national defense strategy (NDS) to implement the president's NSS. The NDS outlines the department's perception of its role in the NSS and how it intends to deal with likely challenges within the context of the NSS. The Joint Chiefs of Staff (JCS) devise an NMS. This, in B. H. Liddell Hart's words, is "policy in execution."[23]

The NMS advises the secretary of defense, the president, and the NSC on the strategic direction of the armed forces. Unlike the NSS and the NDS, the NMS is a standing document that is changed when needed. To offer some strategic stability for financial planning, the NMS applies to program years from two to eight years in the future. It summarizes the global strategic

19

setting, recommends military foundations and strategic principles to support national security objectives, and provides a strategy and force levels that conform to provided fiscal guidance.[24] This inherent disconnect between NSS and NMS processes is worth noting, because it points to the organizational factors that noted security affairs expert Barry Posen asserts "work against integrated strategies." The NSS can ebb and flow with changes of administration, where military strategy is seen as more enduring.[25]

As mentioned previously, military leaders recognize the need for disengagement, and the concept is addressed in the 2004 NMS. That the strategy has not thoroughly considered details of disengagement, however, is apparent. The discussion of disengagement consists of one shallow paragraph, as follows:

> Disengagement. While the force-planning construct assumes that the United States will disengage from some contingencies when faced with a second overlapping campaign, there may be some lesser contingencies that the United States is unwilling or unable to terminate quickly. There may be forces conducting long-term stability operations to reestablish favorable post-conflict security conditions from which the United States cannot disengage. Under such circumstance some important capabilities may not be readily available at the outset of a subsequent conflict. Combatant commanders must consider this possibility when preparing to undertake operations, as many of the same capabilities critical to campaigns are required to conduct lesser contingency operations.[26]

The passive tone of the paragraph indicates that disengagement decisions are distasteful and under the control of others.

Disengagement in Doctrine

According to Posen, "Military doctrine includes the preferred mode of a group of services, a single service, or a subservice for fighting wars. It reflects the judgments of professional military officers, and to a lesser but important extent civilian leaders, about what is and is not militarily possible and necessary."[27] National military strategy is the highest, most general statement of military doctrine. When the NMS is not published, and even in spite of what is published, the NMS can be discovered in force structure, organization, and weapons systems choices.[28] The JCS establishes joint war-fighting doctrine in the form of joint publications. War-termination conditions and end-state objectives are discussed in Joint Publication (JP) 3-0, *Doctrine for Joint Operations*. It is the closest joint doctrine approaches the concept of strategic disengagement. As a component of strategy, JP 3-0 insists joint force commanders "must know how the NCA [National Command Authority] intends to terminate the operation and ensure its outcomes endure, and then determine how to implement that strategic design at the operational level."[29] Joint operations doctrine recognizes that termination design is driven in part by the nature of war itself. Wars over territorial disputes or economic advantage tend to be interest based and to lend themselves to negotiation, persuasion, and coercion. Wars fought in the name of ideology, ethnicity, or religious or cultural primacy tend to be value based and often reflect demands that are seldom negotiable. However, some wars are fought over both value- and interest-based differences.

One critique from the global war on terror and, more specifically, Operation Iraqi Freedom, is that the phases of joint operations outlined in JP 3-0 do not comprehensively reflect the types of operations conducted by military forces. Therefore, the 2006 edition of JP 3-0 expands the phasing model to six phases. Table 2 compares the phases.

Table 2. Evolution of joint operations phasing model

Joint Pub 3-0, 10 Sep 2001	Joint Pub 3-0, 17 Sep 2006
	0: Shape
I: Deter/Engage	I: Deter
II: Seize Initiative	II: Seize Initiative
III: Decisive Operations	III: Dominate
IV: Transition	IV: Stabilize
	V: Enable, Civil Authority

Sources: US Department of Defense, JP 3-0, *Doctrine for Joint Operations* (Washington, DC: US Government Printing Office, 10 September 2001 and 17 September 2006 editions).

Note that the 2001 version includes an explicit engagement phase no longer present in the 2006 version. This certainly does not suggest a need to plan for disengagement. More to the point, neither the 2001 edition nor the 2006 edition includes military disengagement as a phase or as a criterion for another phase.

As alluded to in defining *disengagement*, failing to explicitly include disengagement in operations phasing fosters the current murkiness in defining what is and is not a military role.

If the 2006 publication is an improvement, it is in the buildup to military operations. Phase 0, shaping operations, involves less of the military instrument of power relative to the other instruments. Phase I represents an increase in military involvement, if the threat of military force is the deterrent agent. By phase II, in either version, military forces are engaged, and the military instrument of power is likely predominant. Neither version touches on the key point of disengagement, which involves ratcheting the military instrument back to bring other instruments back to the fore.

Unfortunately, while joint doctrine acknowledges the importance of termination conditions and end-state objectives, doctrine is too far down the strategy hierarchy to bridge strategy to operational design and art. Joint force commanders at the operational level of war depend on clear guidance from above to plan and execute military operations. If a strategic link is missing, it must be between the NSS and the NMS.

Conclusion

Strategic disengagement of military forces falls somewhere in the course of victory and war termination. The challenge for this study is to find its place in American foreign policy. The US military tradition has its roots in what Victor Davis Hanson, classic historian and senior fellow at the Hoover Institute, terms "the Western way of war."[30] This way of thinking about and conducting war is rooted in ancient Greek culture. In Hanson's view, this Greek invention is the historical root of the Powell Doctrine. Just as modern liberal democracy sprang from Greek ideals, both the Western way of war and the Powell Doctrine aim for "an unequivocal, instant resolution to dispute."[31]

When viewed through such a wide historical lens, the tactical disengagement of military forces after victory on the battlefield has not always been relevant or necessary. First, war did not occur on a total, strategic scale until the late eighteenth century saw the confluence of popular conflicts between nation-states with large, professional standing armies. Even then, nation-states kept these large armies abroad to aid their quest to expand empires and annex lands by mainly staying away.

Second, for a nation to release itself from a military obligation, there must be some other interest at play. With large-scale, nation-state wars, interest in disengagement is driven by quagmires or an overextension of the means to an overly ambitious, if not unattainable, end. Quagmire is a prejudicial label applied to long-term involvement in the face of diminishing public support. Overextension generally involves more tasks than force structure or capabilities allow, or alternatively, it creates the existence of higher-priority crises.

Quagmires and overextension are the modern problems that make disengagement relevant. Sir Michael Howard's account of European warfare suggests these factors became truly important with the emergence of populist national wars fought by professional armies. While American independence aligns itself with this period, the modern American problem with disengagement is best studied in the American superpower years since World War II.

Notes

1. Department of Defense, Joint Publication 1-02, *Department of Defense Dictionary of Military and Associated Terms*, 162.

2. See Dictionary.com. *WordNet® 2.1.*

3. See Dictionary.com, *American Heritage® Dictionary of the English Language.*

4. Speier, *Disengagement*, 1.

5. Ibid., 2; and Kennan, *Russia, the Atom, and the West*, 18.

6. Speier, *Disengagement*, 2.

7. Powell, *My American Journey*, 420–21.

8. Speier, *Disengagement*, 9.

9. Howard, *War in European History.*

10. MacArthur, "Farewell Speech."

11. Johnson and Tierney, *Failing to Win*, chap. 1.

12. Collins, "Planning Lessons from Afghanistan and Iraq," 11.

13. Mandel, *Meaning of Military Victory*, 2–3.

14. Ibid., 5. Quote is from Hankey, *Politics, Trials, and Errors*, 26–27, as quoted in Hobbs, *Myth of Victory*, 5.

15. Boule II, "Operational Planning and Conflict Termination," 97–102.

16. Ikenberry, *After Victory*, 257.

17. Ibid., 4.

18. Ibid.

19. Howard, *War in European History*, 140.

20. Ikenberry, *After Victory*, 9.

21. Howard, *War in European History*, 143–44.

22. US Congress, *National Security Act of 1947*.

23. Liddell Hart, *Strategy*, 322.

24. US Department of Defense, *National Defense Strategy of the United States of America*.

25. Posen, *Sources of Military Doctrine*, 226.

26. Chairman, Joint Chiefs of Staff, *National Military Strategy of the United States of America*.

27. Posen, *Sources of Military Doctrine*, 14.

28. Ibid.

29. US Department of Defense, JP 3-0, *Doctrine for Joint Operations*.

30. Hanson, *Western Way of War*. Hanson characterizes it as "a collision of soldiers on an open plain in a magnificent display of courage, skill, physical prowess, honor, and fair play, and a concomitant repugnance for decoy, ambush, sneak attacks, and the involvement of noncombatants." See also McGrath, "Western Way of War: From Plato to NATO," 13–15.

31. Keegan, introduction to Hanson, *Western Way of War*, xii.

Chapter 3

Disengagement in the Cold War

*U.S. strategic thought is really a product of World War II
and the post-war world. For most of American history,
the U.S. military did not need to formulate grand strategy.
Since World War II, much work has been done on nuclear
strategy and policy, but conventional strategy and policy
have suffered from inadequate attention.*

—Senate Armed Services Committee Staff Report
Defense Organization: The Need for Change

This chapter considers how strategic military disengagement
decisions are influenced by US national security strategy. Specifically, it examines the supposed necessary congruence between the NSS and its subordinate national military strategy.
Historical national security strategies of the Cold War (1945–90)
are outlined and related to their concurrent national military
strategies. Relevant conflicts of the period are used to examine
the congruence and appropriateness of the NMS to the NSS.

Organization is based on presidencies. For each presidential
administration, the defining NSS and NMS are briefly explained.
Relevant, though not necessarily all inclusive, conflicts are used
as minicases and focus on opportunities that existed for strategic military disengagement, including when and how the United
States tried to disengage and how various attempts fared.

The Cold War

The context of the conflicts is critical; so, some background
is necessary. The range and depth of review vary by conflict,
but basic points for consideration include the type and basis of
the conflict, how it started, and how it was fought. When relevant, the analysis may consider how the United States became
engaged and the order and pace at which ground, air, and naval forces were committed.

In examining disengagement, this study examines whether
termination criteria and end-state objectives were met, the ul-

timate terms of disengagement, and whether the operation was deemed a victory. Providing policy makers with an understanding of what has and has not worked historically may help determine future decisions.

With varying degrees of coherency, presidential policies reflect the NSS. Some noteworthy strategies, whether due to the events of the day or the personality of the president, are known as the president's doctrine (i.e., Monroe Doctrine, Truman Doctrine). For analysis, the years of US national strategy since World War II are further divided into the Cold War and post–Cold War eras.

Distinguished national security scholar Robert Art groups US grand strategic options generically into seven approaches (fig. 1). He discusses the approaches in a contemporary context, but this study uses the taxonomy for historical US national security strategies. First is isolationism, representing the lowest level of international engagement. Military disengagement aims for the absolute. Second on the continuum is cooperative security, whereby limiting other states' offensive capabilities reduces the occurrence of war. Third is regional collective security, where international engagement is increased but is focused closely on the primary sphere of US interests–Europe. Strategic military disengagement is not a major factor because it counters the soft-power priorities of forward presence in allied countries and because of the limited breadth of deployments.

Deployments expand as the NSS arrives at containment, the fourth option, though breadth of deployment is still partly determined by the nature of the enemy. This realm, holding the line against aggressor states, defined US national security

Figure 1. Possible approaches to US grand strategy. (Reprinted from Robert J. Art, *A Grand Strategy for America* (Ithaca, NY: Cornell University Press, 2003). Figure is this author's interpretation of Dr. Art's discussion. Any inaccuracy in the depiction is unintentional.

strategy in the Cold War. The breadth was large, as the enemy was global communism. Large, standing armies became a requirement, and disengagement was still contrary to the emphasis on forward presence for the maintenance of a timely and credible threat of counterintervention. The fifth option, selective engagement, intervenes only in those conflicts that pose a threat to the country's long-term interests. Depending on the nature of the threat, this strategy may be more or less expansive than containment. When this option is more expansive, strategic military disengagement becomes increasingly important, as long-term interventions constrain the president's ability to choose to intervene in concurrent crises. The criticality of disengagement continues to grow across the rest of the continuum for the same reasons. Under a strategy of global collective security, the sixth option, the United States and its allies attempt to keep the peace everywhere; so, timely disengagement of military force is crucial. The seventh and final option, dominion, is as unrealistic extreme as is isolation. Forcibly trying to remake the world in America's own image suggests a reach into imperialism that none but the most hard-core zealots would recommend or would accuse the United States of attempting.[1]

Containment, Deterrence, and Counterintervention

Since World War II, denoting US presidents' national security strategies as doctrines has become standard practice. Pres. Harry S. Truman formally issued the Truman Doctrine in a speech to Congress on 12 March 1947. Codified in National Security Council 68, Truman's speech committed the United States to freedom worldwide and set the basis for US national security strategy for the duration of the Cold War. His so-called *containment order* rallied Americans to the new struggle against the perils of world communism.[2] The Truman Doctrine set the orientation on which the bureaucratic and military organizations that make up the US national security apparatus were built.[3]

Harry Truman: Containment and Deterrence

The NMS under Truman was dominated by nuclear deterrence, as was true throughout the Cold War. The conventional component was characterized by the perception that the Soviets or Chinese communists would subsume their weak neighbors, thus requiring a tough US counterintervention stance.[4] Table 3 outlines the evolution of the NSS and the NMS since World War II.

The hallmark military conflict of the Truman administration was the Korean War. If disengagement is about releasing oneself from a commitment, that commitment to Korea was made in the Cairo Declaration of 1943. The United States, the United

Table 3. US strategies and conflicts since World War II

President	NSS	NMS	Conflicts
Truman	Containment	Deterrence	Korea
Eisenhower	New Look Containment	Deterrence	Korea Vietnam
Kennedy	Containment and Reversal	Deterrence Flexible Response	Cuban missile crisis Vietnam
Johnson	Containment	Deterrence	Vietnam
Nixon	Containment Détente	Deterrence	Vietnam
Carter	Containment	Deterrence	Iran
Reagan	Containment Rollback	Deterrence	Lebanon Grenada Libya Iran
GHW Bush	Multilateral Engagement	Deter and Defeat	Panama Iraq
Clinton	Engagement and Enlargement	Flexible and Selective Engagement	Somalia Bosnia Kosovo Korea Iraq Sudan/ Afghanistan
GW Bush	Preemption	Preemption	GWOT Afghanistan Iraq

Source: Author's original conceptualization.

Kingdom, and China committed to a free and independent Korea, which was at the time under Japanese occupation. This commitment was reaffirmed on 26 July 1945 at the Potsdam Conference.[5] Korea never was officially divided through diplomatic conferences as was Germany, though some reports have Pres. Franklin D. Roosevelt and Soviet premier Joseph Stalin informally making such an arrangement at Potsdam. This reasoning casts the Moscow Conference in December 1945 as cementing Stalin's understanding that the Soviets would control Korea north of the 38th parallel.[6] Most evidence suggests the decision was pragmatic, however, as the Soviets already had forces in Korea to accept Japan's surrender, and the United States did not. Essentially, viewing possession as nine-tenths of the law, the Soviets chose to view their 38th parallel occupation line as a de facto military delimitation.[7]

The United States, the United Kingdom, and China proceeded toward Korean independence, under auspices of the UN. The Soviets rejected UN jurisdiction, arguing the UN had no say in the conclusion of peace treaties. After elections were held, the government of the Republic of Korea was established on 15 August 1948 and was validated by the UN in December 1948. A UN General Assembly resolution, issued 12 December 1948, recommended occupation forces be withdrawn from Korea "as early as practicable."[8] The Soviets announced their complete withdrawal in December 1948, but they never allowed independent confirmation. The UN confirmed that the United States completed the withdrawal of its occupation forces on 29 June 1949.[9]

The prompt and successful disengagement of US forces from Korea, just as the occupation agreement, was pragmatic. Congress viewed the containment era as one of weapons, specifically nuclear weapons, and not personnel. Because of drastically dwindling budgets, by 1947, the JCS had officially deemed Korea not of vital interest to national security. This was echoed by Secretary of State Dean Acheson in a January 1950 speech in which he pointedly left Korea out of the US defense perimeter in the Far East.[10]

Thus, the disengagement of US military forces may be viewed as the removal of a deterrent to North Korea's intent to unify the peninsula by force. This end state was shared by South

Korea and the UN, though by disengaging foreign military forces, the UN hoped to achieve the end of unification through diplomatic means. Throughout 1949, the United Nations Commission on Korea repeatedly tried to get the Soviets to honor the terms of the joint US-Soviet commission, per the Moscow Conference, but to no avail. The commission noted dangerous trends in the security arrangement that could not be eased as long as the Soviets resisted UN efforts to confirm the withdrawal of Soviet forces from the North.[11]

With US forces disengaged and border conflicts becoming more acute, the tipping point appeared in the South's May 1950 national assembly elections. The 85 percent turnover rate of incumbent delegates exposed the Republic of Korea's government as illegitimate and vulnerable. On 20 June 1950, the Democratic People's Republic of Korea government issued a call for a unified election—without UN involvement.[12] The first report of a breach of the peace came five days later on 25 June 1950. The objectives stated in the subsequent UN Security Council resolution included the immediate cessation of hostilities and the withdrawal of North Korean armed forces to the 38th parallel.[13]

America's first successful strategic military disengagement was thus reversed on 27 June 1950, when President Truman ordered US air and sea forces to "cover and support" Korean government troops.[14] Two days later, American ground forces were added to the order.[15] Telling of the rationale for reengaging in Korea, only the introductory paragraph of President Truman's statement dealt with Korea. The remaining three-quarters addressed the threat of global communism to Formosa (Taiwan) and the Philippines and the "acceleration . . . of military assistance to the forces of France and the Associated States in Indochina and the dispatch of a military mission."[16]

Noted Stanford international relations scholar Alexander George questioned the effect of engaging ground forces so quickly. He wondered in retrospect if air and naval forces were enough to offset the threat while avoiding the "irreversible commitment" inherent in ground-force action. In his view, the question of which types of force were used is important because "the character and development of the Korean War were determined to a considerable extent by the decision to use US ground forces to stem the advancing North Koreans and, eventually, to roll them back."[17] Apparently, such alternatives were not considered, despite the traditional military view that "ground forces should not become involved in a war on the Asian continent."[18]

The second engagement in Korea shows that having an end state in mind is not the same as planning for disengagement. The US military intervention seemed successful after the landing at Inchon. Allied forces had a clear end state of restoring the status quo ante: the 38th parallel would be restored as the border between North and South Korea. Clearly, concisely, and militarily achievable, this end state presented itself by the end of September 1950.

Then, on 1 October 1950, in perhaps the classic example of overextension in the face of military success, Gen Douglas MacArthur decided to extend his mission from the UN mandate to push the overwhelmed and retreating North Korean Peoples Army all the way to the Yalu River. He wanted to use his military means to solve the political problem of reunifying the Korean peninsula.[19] Unification was no longer the objective, but operations were driving national and international objectives. On 7 October, the UN General Assembly issued a new resolution expanding the objectives in Korea, which included stability throughout Korea and UN-sanctioned elections for a unified Korea.[20] The first was a daunting military task. The second was impossible through military means alone.

After reaching the Yalu River in November 1950, UN forces were compelled to retreat because of China's entry into the conflict. MacArthur again pressed both publicly and politically for expansion of the conflict, and President Truman relieved him of command. When MacArthur stated "there is no substitute for victory," Truman responded with the new military objectives "to repel attack and to restore peace."[21]

Before MacArthur forfeited disengagement with his push north of the 38th parallel, clear military victory, according to the original objective, was achieved. Without venturing too far into the counterfactual, it is not absurd to speculate there also was a real chance at a World War I–style negotiated peace, where US allies in Asia and Europe would have found assurance that collective security was indeed meaningful and where up to 80 percent of US casualties would have been avoided.[22]

Instead, by overreaching the original end state, the allies drew China into the war and wasted two more years and thousands of lives to recover to the point of departure.[23]

After avoiding being pushed off the peninsula by the Chinese, the United States saw the next opportunity for disengagement with a semblance of victory in March 1951, when allied forces again had pushed Chinese and North Korean forces back to the 38th parallel. Now, officials in Washington opted to call for a cease-fire, hoping to reach an acceptable settlement near the June 1950 status quo. Unfortunately, General MacArthur, again operating under his exceptional view of the role of a theater commander, publicly demanded a cease-fire quite different from the proposal being coordinated in Washington. Washington had reverted to the end-state objectives of 27 June 1950. MacArthur continued, at least in effect, to operate under the more expansive end-state objectives of 7 October 1950. Again, his reach exceeded his grasp, this time in the use of non-military instruments of power. MacArthur leveraged threats of sanctions, which neither the United States nor the United Nations intended to apply, for an objective—reunification—long abandoned by both Washington and the UN.[24]

On the ground, politicians on both sides realized "at about the same time that *neither* of us could quit *nor* win" (emphasis in original).[25] Right or wrong, General MacArthur believed this idea of limited force in war was alien. In congressional testimony after being relieved of command, MacArthur said "the concept that I have is that when you go into war, you have exhausted all other potentialities of bringing the disagreements to an end."[26] Once engaged, limiting force, in MacArthur's view, was appeasement; he was right, at least within the military culture and types of wars that framed his career. When war is total, or existential, as the world wars were, there is no substitute for victory.

Korea, though fought by the conventional means MacArthur had mastered, was not total war for the United States. Rather, it was a stand to let the Soviets know they could not expand unchallenged, as Japan had done in Manchuria in 1931 and Germany in the Sudetenland in 1938.[27] It was difficult for everyone—whether soldier, politician, or public citizen—to accept the nonvictory and nondefeat of Korea. "It was the first modern war . . . fought with no clear end in view as we waged it, no known geographical goal at which someone would blow a whistle and it would all be over."[28]

If expanding the objectives by going into North Korea was the key mistake of the war, next in line may have been President Truman's decision in June 1951 to "accept the Communist demand for the cessation of hostilities prior to the opening of truce negotiations."[29] Had the United States followed the example from World War I of continuing the offensive until the armistice was actually signed, it may have ended the war in the summer of 1951 and avoided Mao Tse-tung's conversion to the *talking while fighting* strategy that dragged the negotiations and bloodshed out over two years, eroding American political will. Ceasing offensive operations too soon made it difficult, and ultimately impossible, to disengage military forces. A stalemated fight, in perpetual cease-fire, with an armed, capable, and recuperated enemy, requires a military presence as a deterrent to resumption of hostilities. When the United Nations and the United States negotiated an armistice with North Korea, its inability to disengage military forces was the agreed-upon price to pay for an end to the carnage of a stalemate. Maintenance of the cease-fire replaced the reunification promises of Potsdam, Yalta, and Moscow as the front-burner issue between the United States and the Soviets. Strategic military disengagement is conceptually antithetical to containment, a concept based on a regional and local balance of power.

Seyom Brown, noted international relations author and professor, saw this balance-of-power view of containment as an expansionist NSS, noting, "The Korean War thus marked a globalization of containment (every place had significant weight in the power balance) in terms of operational commitments as well as rhetoric. The United States finally 'intervened' physically in the Chinese Civil War by interposing the Seventh Fleet between Mao Tse-tung's forces and Chiang's last island fortresses. Despite our anti-colonial protestations, we now put our money behind the French efforts to suppress the Ho Chi Minh Communist-nationalist insurgency in Indochina."[30]

The containment order clearly was Truman's greatest legacy to US national security in the Cold War. Yet, several other events in Truman's term eventually would lead to US involvement in

Vietnam, which was by far the largest disengagement dilemma the United States faced in the Cold War era. Like Korea, the Potsdam Conference split Vietnam into two occupation sectors, manned by the Chinese in the north and the British in the south. While US forces were not involved in the occupation, US interests became collaterally tied to Vietnam through collective security arrangements. Proving the credibility and viability of collective security, specifically in the guise of the United Nations and the North Atlantic Treaty Organization, pushed Truman to contradict President Roosevelt's policy under the Atlantic Charter of self-determination for all nations. Though reasons varied in the North and South, the results were the same: disengagement of occupation forces and the resumption of French colonial rule. Truman resisted direct involvement until after China fell to communism in 1949, and then finally North Korea invaded South Korea. As mentioned previously, the situation in Korea led Truman to commit the first advisors to Vietnam. Though the Military Assistance Advisory Group (MAAG) started with only four advisors on the ground, the US was on what would become a slippery slope of commitment to Vietnam.

Dwight Eisenhower: New Look Containment and Deterrence

The Truman Doctrine dominated the Cold War era, but succeeding presidents did tweak the strategy of containment. Pres. Dwight D. Eisenhower took a more *long-haul* view of containment, believing the US stand against Soviet communism would have to be economically sustainable.[31] Nuclear deterrence continued to dominate NMS. In fact, Eisenhower's massive retaliation strategy served the conventional purpose of signaling the Soviets that direct conventional responses to aggression, such as happened in Korea, were by no means necessary. The United States reserved the right "to respond massively, with nuclear weapons, at a place and time of its choosing."[32]

Despite signals of massive retaliation, low-intensity conflicts in contested Third World or post-colonial states were becoming the stage for superpower rivalry safe from nuclear escalation. What became the Eisenhower Doctrine evolved through his presidency. It was given in a message to Congress on 5 January

1957 and stated that the United States would use armed forces upon request in response to imminent or actual aggression to the United States; and, more importantly, that the United States would give various forms of aid to countries that stood against the spread of communism. Eisenhower ended the active conflict in Korea, but he could not disengage US military forces in the face of the overwhelming numerical superiority of North Korean forces.

When president-elect Eisenhower first toured Korea, the war was stalemated at the 38th parallel, with troops dying while peace negotiations dragged. Still, he was told by the Army generals on the ground that the United States and the United Nations could, given enough men and supplies, push the enemy all the way back to the Yalu River. Alternatively, enemy lines could be broken and North Korean forces attrited, though at a cost of roughly 50,000 more casualties. More men and equipment then would be required for follow-on operations. "Generals are paid to fight, not to think up reasons for *avoiding* a fight," so their natural inclination was to inform Eisenhower on how the war could be continued, if not won, not how it could be ended (emphasis in original).[33] President Eisenhower instead chose to negotiate an armistice. While it did not fully disengage US military forces, it ended the carnage and preserved US military strength, national power, and will. Put another way, it sacrificed strategic victory for a strategy that preserved some continuing advantage on the broader world stage.

In terms of end-state objectives and termination criteria, US military strategy in Korea was an improvisation. American NSS was almost entirely focused on Europe and included neither military options in Korea, specifically, nor viable military strategies for limited wars in general.[34] In the eventual armistice, the end state, per the 27 June 1950 resolution, was successful, though it arguably took longer than it might have and cost more lives than it should have. If the immediate objective of the war was to preserve the integrity of South Korea against communist expansion, it was successful. More importantly though, it helped establish a baseline for the Cold War, whereby the United States served notice to the Soviets that aggression would not go unchecked by the West. Both sides limited their possible military means to stay short of a nuclear threshold. By rejecting the possibility of total victory over the Chinese or the Soviets, at the risk of a third world war, the United States traded strategic military disengagement for the relative peace of a stable armistice that preserved the status quo.[35]

One lesson regarding disengagement, suggested by the Korean experience, is that *disengaging too soon increases the likelihood of subsequent engagements.* It is reasonable to suggest that the United States disengaged forces prematurely in 1949, without confirmation of the Soviet status in the North. Referring to Speier's tenets of disengagement, the 1949 disengagement arguably would fail on all points. First, while there was bilateral action, there was no credible assurance. Second, without said assurance, the United States forced disengagement while North Korea still posed a credible threat, as evidenced by near-continuous border incursions from 1948 to 1950. Third, disengagement decisions clearly were not based on present or future intentions, as there was scant evidence to suggest policies of peaceful coexistence from the North.[36] If there were an advantage to early disengagement, however, it was in leaving options open. At least *the nation gets to decide anew each encounter, vice being committed already.* In ignoring other opportunities for disengagement, the United States deepened the commitment to stay and made further loss of lives a fait accompli.

While President Eisenhower avoided new major military engagements in his administration, he also failed to disengage from two conflicts that ultimately would define the Cold War. Where Truman first committed advisors to Indochina in 1950 as a response to North Korea's invasion of South Korea, the end state in Korea, coupled with Eisenhower's growing fear of the domino effect, laid the groundwork for US involvement in Vietnam. By 1954 the MAAG was up to 342 advisors.[37]

John Kennedy: Containment, Reversal, and Deterrence

The Kennedy Doctrine continued support for the containment of communism and specifically added the reversal of communist progress in the Western Hemisphere. Nuclear deterrence strategy continued to carry the day, as it had under Truman and Eisenhower, but Kennedy backed away from *massive retaliation* in favor of *flexible response*, which proposed to meet violence at the level at which it was initiated. In his inaugural address on 20 January 1961, President Kennedy warned, "Let every nation know, whether it wishes us well or ill, that we shall pay any price, bear any burden, meet any hardship, support any friend, oppose any foe, in order to assure the survival and the success of liberty."[38] While it is beyond the scope of this study to determine causality, it seems the change of strategy and Kennedy's rhetoric could account for the increased number of conflicts in his short term as compared to Eisenhower's two terms.

Kennedy and his defense experts argued massive retaliation was not a credible deterrent for small actions. For support, they cited Ho Chi Minh's victory in North Vietnam over the French in 1954 and Red China's shelling of Matsu and Quemoy in the first (1954) and second (1958) Taiwan Strait crises, none of which triggered a response.[39] The counter to Kennedy's interpretation, and of particular interest to the discussion of disengagement, lies in the fact that Eisenhower's conservative use of the military instrument of power, particularly ground forces, resulted in eight years with no disengagement dilemmas. Conversely, Kennedy's military strategy was tested in Cuba, and his decision to commit significant numbers of advisors in Vietnam started the United States on the slippery slope to 540,000 troops on the ground with little in the way of strategic objectives.

The Cuban missile crisis is the conflict most closely associated with the Kennedy administration. While it is the extreme case of nuclear brinksmanship to date, in the context of this study, it was a direct military conflict. Taken in total, the missile crisis was one act in an ongoing drama involving US efforts to overthrow Fidel Castro and Soviet efforts to lend credibility to its inferior nuclear missile capabilities by placing "nukes" in America's backyard. Taken in relative isolation from the rest of the drama, as a study in strategic military disengagement, the key is that President Kennedy chose a naval blockade of Cuba and opted against a ground invasion or even air strikes.

US airpower was used to provide the intelligence proof Kennedy needed to confront Nikita Khrushchev before he could unveil the missiles as a fait accompli.[40] With photo proof from Central Intelligence Agency (CIA) U-2 and US Air Force F-101 aircraft, Kennedy consulted with the executive committee of the NSC (ExComm). Six lines of action were considered: do nothing, apply diplomatic pressure, secretly approach Castro, conduct a surgical air strike to destroy all of the missiles, a full-scale invasion, or blockade the island. Recognizing that while the crisis was primarily political, Kennedy realized there would have to be a military component, with the ultimate plan to include at least one of the last three. The joint chiefs unanimously believed that air strikes and an invasion were required. Kennedy was sure either, and certainly both combined, would lead to escalation, if not in Cuba, then in Berlin. Kennedy thus opted for the blockade, strongly advocated by Secretary of Defense Robert S. McNamara, as strong, yet limited, with the United States retaining the most control of the situation.[41]

By choosing a comparatively low-scale form of engagement, Kennedy believed disengagement was easy when the Soviets complied with US demands that existing missiles be dismantled and shipped back to the Soviet Union. First, the use of naval forces allowed quick intervention. Second, it minimized the risk of confrontation by exposing only large capital ships to harm. The Soviets could kill a handful of ground troops or shoot down a couple of airplanes without crossing the threshold. Sinking hundreds of millions of dollars worth of US national treasure, not to mention killing scores of American crew members on board, is a wholly different proposition. Third, when Khrushchev relented, the spigot of naval power was easy to turn off.

Ultimately, *the form of engagement, coupled with a clear end state, kept the crisis in check*. Thus, a diplomatic, economic, and information campaign that would have taken years to bear fruit, if it ever did, was instead averted within two weeks, from 16 to 28 October 1962. Lest too much be made of the compelling power of the blockade, Graham Allison points out that ultimately, it took the credible threat of more action, specifically air strikes and invasion, to compel the Soviets to remove the missiles.[42]

Cuba showed that even when the stakes are extraordinarily high, the degree of engagement of military forces determines the ease of disengagement. Still, the easiest conflict from which to disengage is the one in which the military never was engaged.

In this regard, flexible response was a much more expansive NSS than massive retaliation. By comparison, massive retaliation focused on a more fiscally efficient approach that limited military engagement to only the most vital of national interests. The irony for military strategy was that while Army culture was more in line with Eisenhower's philosophy on the use of military force on a large scale, and as a last resort, military leaders were more inclined to accept Kennedy's increased military budgets, though the president's strategy of fighting brushfire wars in the Third World was diametrically opposed to what Andrew Krepinevich terms "the Army concept."[43]

That Kennedy's NSS was more expansive is further evidenced by the variety of engagements it fostered. While Cuba represented the epitome of Cold War superpower rivalry through nuclear brinksmanship, at the other end of the spectrum of conflict was the growing insurgency in South Vietnam. This end of the spectrum better explains Kennedy's flexible response strategy. Even as a senator touring Indochina and studying French counterinsurgency efforts in Vietnam and Algeria, Kennedy apparently believed insurgencies were the most likely wars under the nuclear umbrella. As president, with the added impetus of Khrushchev's announcement of Soviet support for "national wars of liberation," Kennedy pushed his view through the national security apparatus. Kennedy's top-down approach did little to turn Army culture, and while Vietnam gradually gained stature as the most likely place for a test of Kennedy's NSS, the Army's convictions kept it focused on a large conventional war in Europe. Most of the Kennedy administration's efforts focused on organizational and budgetary issues, with no real attempts to fix the core problems in doctrine or the development of an integrated interagency approach to insurgency. Without such an overarching focus or a competent agent at the executive level to enforce it on the agencies and services, the Army paid lip service to President Kennedy's demands for force-structure changes aimed at counterinsurgency.[44]

The NMS of flexible response did not prove so troublesome to the Air Force. Nuclear deterrence strategy maintained primacy, and that was the Strategic Air Command's forte. In terms of Vietnam specifically, and President Kennedy's unconventional warfare focus generally, Air Force culture was less affronted.

First, counterinsurgency is traditionally viewed as better served by ground tactics. Direct support to ground troops was culturally a secondary mission to the Air Force, and close air support to ground forces remains essentially the same, regardless of the enemy's nature or tactics. Second, the Air Force's primary role of strategic attack aligned with the Kennedy administration's view of the proper antidote for the counterinsurgency in Vietnam. Walt Rostow, deputy to the president's special assistant for national security, believed strategic bombing of North Vietnam was the way to influence the source of the insurgency.[45]

The military was not alone in its lack of consensus. In the advisory years, while there was debate over policy, passions were not as inflamed. The policy deliberation that ultimately led to the February 1965 decision to commit combat troops actually began in the late summer of 1963. As the Saigon government deteriorated, the way ahead for the United States was by no means clear. It was time to dramatically escalate US commitment or to leave altogether.[46] During what University of California professor Frederik Logevall terms "the long 1964," US officials "chose war over disengagement despite deep doubts about the war's prospects and about Vietnam's importance to US security and over the opposition of important voices in the Congress, in the press, and in the world community."[47] The conventional wisdom for explaining this decision is the "inevitability thesis": to argue that US officials had the opportunity to disengage requires that they had a real, practical choice. Most analysts agree that by 1964 the United States was too committed for any president to radically reorient US policy to disengagement.[48]

Logevall is not alone in countering conventional wisdom. At least at the start of the long 1964, there seemed to be no consensus on escalation. According to James Galbraith, son of President Kennedy's ambassador to Vietnam, the president planned and had nearly set in motion efforts to withdraw American advisors from Vietnam without the prerequisite of victory. Kennedy based his plan on the recommendations, in a 2 October 1963 report, of a mission to Saigon by Secretary McNamara and Gen Maxwell Taylor, chairperson of the JCS. McNamara and Taylor recommended the "Defense Department should announce in the very near future presently prepared plans to withdraw 1,000 out of 17,000 U.S. military personnel stationed in Vietnam by the end of 1963." This intent was formalized in National Security Action Memorandum (NSAM) 263 on 11 October 1963. Unfortunately, President Kennedy, hoisted on the petard of his own "bear any burden" rhetoric, chose to keep the move low-key and was assassinated before the plan was implemented. Galbraith points to subtle changes within Pres. Lyndon B. Johnson's NSAM 273, which, counter to conventional wisdom, veered away from Kennedy's apparent Vietnam policy. Galbraith argues the changes in NSAM 273 opened the way for the military and the CIA to implement a seaborne sabotage campaign against North Vietnam that directly led to the Gulf of Tonkin incident and America's escalation of the war in Vietnam.[49]

Whether or not President Kennedy had resolved to get American forces out of Vietnam at any cost is open for debate. Of interest to this study is his withdrawal-without-victory strategy. Though arguably on the table had Kennedy survived, it was not in fact implemented. Galbraith points out a potential divergence of NMS from President Kennedy's strategy, considering it "well known that the Pentagon did not favor withdrawal."[50] He assumes the military and the CIA thus looked for loopholes in the president's instructions, finding their way ahead eased in the wake of Kennedy's assassination.[51]

Lyndon Johnson: Containment and Deterrence and Vietnam

President Johnson largely carried out the Kennedy Doctrine. The distinguishing trait of the Johnson Doctrine was its declaration in 1965 that revolutions in the Western Hemisphere would be considered of American interest when their object was the establishment of a communist regime. Johnson's focus was on the Great Society. His national security policy was consumed with Vietnam.

If President Kennedy had indeed planned to withdraw US forces from Vietnam, as James Galbraith asserts, keeping it secret for political and diplomatic reasons ironically forced continued engagement. President Johnson could not publicly announce a withdrawal-without-victory strategy close on the heels of Kennedy's assassination. Kennedy had first introduced substantial numbers of ground troops in Vietnam in 1962, and Johnson continued Kennedy's policies, incrementally. When Johnson finally committed combat troops in 1965, it was to "buy time" for the government of South Vietnam. Johnson faced the same dilemma Kennedy had in disengaging US forces. Domestic politics have a large impact on foreign policy, and thus disengagement. Domestically, the president could not appear soft on communism. The Democrats had lost China to the communists and nearly Korea as well. Thus, Johnson followed Eisenhower's Korea playbook, hoping US forces could hold off Ho Chi Minh long enough for the government of South Vietnam to build itself up to Korean status in terms of coping with the insurgency.[52]

The 1968 Tet offensive, the closest thing to a decisive victory on the battlefield, provided the best semblance to a classic opportunity to declare victory and disengage US military forces. The Vietcong were practically wiped out, and the North Vietnamese Army suffered massive losses in personnel and equipment from which it took years to recover. "Tet was a victory in the eyes of the Army leadership because it advanced the accomplishment of its goals," claims Krepinevich. The Army culture was based on large-scale, firepower-intensive, conventional set-piece battle, which Krepinevich terms the *Army concept*. The destruction of up to 58,000 enemy troops and tons of heavy equipment during Tet amounts to perfect metrics within the Army concept strategy of attrition.[53] Even from the North Vietnamese perspective at the time, Gen Vo Nguyen Giap was reportedly devastated, as the offensive had failed both militarily and politically in kicking off an uprising in South Vietnam.[54] Ironically, it was the minimal goal of Tet, arguably rationalized after the fact, which met success. The North Vietnamese created chaos, then urged Johnson to halt bombing and start negotiations. The classic communist fighting and talking tactic, effective in Korea, served its purpose again. Though almost all communist gains were reversed within hours or days, with even Hue being completely liberated in about a month, the spike in Americans killed during Tet tipped the already tenuous balance of American popular will.[55] Johnson cited accurate reports of the North's perception of their crushing defeat, but he had lost credibility with the public after the surprise of Tet.

In early March 1968, President Johnson was considering a buildup of 206,000 troops, spreading ground battles into Laos and Cambodia, and lifting bombing constraints. Within a few short weeks, Johnson took all that off the table, replaced Gen William C. Westmoreland, announced he would not run for re-election, and stopped bombing. One telling observation in this time came from a 15 March lunch meeting that President Johnson had with Dean Acheson, who noted that there was "no correlation between the military objectives and the time and resources available to the U.S. to accomplish them."[56]

In short, Johnson established a plan for strategic military disengagement. Unfortunately, by this time public opinion was so negative he was unable to spin the events into victory; instead, he began a *peace offensive* in hopes of salvaging a withdrawal without defeat. Again, as had happened in Korea, fighting while talking led to more troops dying over the next five years than had died in the preceding five.[57]

Richard Nixon: Containment and Deterrence

The Nixon Doctrine, largely influenced by the Vietnam War, was conducive to military disengagement. The quagmire of Vietnam led to a serious change in US policy. Under Nixon, the United States would provide a nuclear umbrella for its allies and would fight for vital interests with air and sea power and financial aid but affected allies would be expected to provide the bulk of land forces.[58] The means Nixon used to disengage from Vietnam, and the resultant overthrow of the South Vietnamese government in 1975, contributed to the negative connotation of disengagement. The NMS under Nixon, reflecting the country's fatigue with Vietnam, was rather clearly United States first and aimed to limit American military exposure abroad.

After Tet, beginning with President Johnson and accelerating under President Nixon, American strategy in Vietnam was effectively limited to the discussion of how to get US forces out. While the marginal levels of the threats, both internal and external, to the South Vietnamese government were reduced after Tet, they both still existed and would only recover in the absence of US forces. Such a *cut-and-run* approach is the least

43

favorable type of disengagement, again violating all of Speier's tenets of disengagement.

As a candidate for president, Nixon ran on a promise of "peace with honor," having ruled out a "military victory" in Vietnam, but neither did he intend to be "the first president of the United States to lose a war."[59] Nixon and his national security advisor, Henry A. Kissinger, shared the view that there could be no victory in Vietnam, but their visions differed on what could be aimed for. Nixon sought a durable peace, not a Korea-style armistice. Kissinger hoped to reach an agreement that would give the South Vietnamese a "reasonable" chance to survive for a "decent interval."[60]

Nixon first tried a linkage strategy, seeking to link warming diplomatic ties with the Soviet Union to their leveraging concessions from the North Vietnamese. The Soviets did not bite, however, preferring détente with the United States unencumbered by Vietnam ties. Vietnamization thus emerged; the United States would withdraw ground troops, leaving trained and equipped South Vietnamese in their places. Nixon did not intend to disengage completely (i.e., cut and run) but rather sought to gain the release of prisoners and quell domestic unrest caused by the large troop presence, while continuing to bolster the security of South Vietnam with US airpower.[61] Nixon's informal floating of this idea to reporters in July 1969 ultimately resulted in the *furnish-your-own-troops* Nixon Doctrine.

The Vietnamization process reduced US troop strength in Vietnam in 1969 from 549,500 to 484,000; by 1 May 1972 only 69,000 remained. Combat deaths dropped 95 percent in the same period, and war expenditures dropped by two-thirds. Melvin Laird's final report as secretary of defense in 1973 stated: "Vietnamization . . . today is virtually completed. As a consequence of the success of the military aspects of Vietnamization, the South Vietnamese people today, in my view, are fully capable of providing for their own in-country security against the North Vietnamese."[62]

Whether or not one accepts Laird's assessment, Vietnamization cannot be viewed alone, but it must be viewed in the context of the entire Nixon program. Kissinger, whom Nixon directed to revitalize the NSC, orchestrated the program. He organized the NSC so that he chaired multiple committees, effectively making himself the gatekeeper and placing himself in control of all recommendations flowing to President Nixon.[63] Vietnamization was the military piece, supplemented by a two-pronged diplomatic approach that included the Paris peace talks and additional secret negotiations Kissinger himself held with North Vietnamese officials in Paris. Indeed, the Linebacker II bombing campaign showed America's continuing resolve despite ground force withdrawals. This forced the North Vietnamese to the peace table, where the combination of open and secret talks led to an agreement. The Paris Peace Accords, signed on 27 January 1973, included the complete withdrawal of US forces within 60 days.[64] Of note, the agreement said nothing about withdrawal of North Vietnamese forces from the South. Reflecting on Speier's tenets of disengagement, US disengagement was agreed upon bilaterally, but its execution was unilateral.

Most analysts and historians view Vietnam as a defeat for the United States. Still, a variety of arguments rationalizes the US victory. Laird, for his part, does not deny the ultimate US defeat, but he quibbles over its necessity and who is to blame. In a 2005 essay in *Foreign Affairs*, Laird argues the United States had not lost in 1973 when the last ground forces withdrew. Defeat did not come until the US Congress cut off funding for South Vietnam to continue its fight. By waiting so long and allowing public support to erode so far, once the troop withdrawal got started, Laird maintained, it developed its own momentum and could not stop with the withdrawal of ground forces. The Paris Peace Accords allowed both the United States and the Soviet Union to continue funding their allies at a specified level, essentially replacing arms and equipment. Laird cited recently released North Vietnamese records that showed the Soviets never honored the pact, sending over $1 billion a year in military aid to Hanoi. The US Congress, conversely, barely sent the allowed amount and stopped that after two years. South Vietnam held for those two years and peace talks continued, until the day in 1975 when the US Congress cut off funds. At that point, the North left the peace talks, never returned, and soon thereafter invaded and overran the South.[65]

Thus, the point Laird makes is that Vietnam was not lost because of strategic military disengagement (i.e., Vietnamization) but rather through complete disengagement of all elements of national power. For this, Laird asserts, the Congress, the president, the secretary of state, and the secretary of defense must share the blame.

Even deeper and at the core of the problem, especially from the public opinion standpoint, end-state objectives never were used effectively in the quarter-century the United States was involved in Vietnam. When combat forces were engaged in 1965, no clear, militarily achievable objectives were given. Political leaders had opportunities to capitalize on military successes to disengage had that been the desire. The longer decision makers waited, the longer the war of attrition continued and the more difficult the decision became to disengage without decisive victory.[66] Another takeaway in terms of disengagement is that the more objectives depend on others, the less likely will be their accomplishments. Depending on troops from the army of the Republic of Vietnam and the Ngo Dinh Diem government or subsequent governments to achieve US objectives with meaning was frustrating. Kissinger argues that the United States can *declare victory* anytime we want by defining victory according to already accomplished objectives. Truly achieving that victory, however, is more likely if the objectives depend directly on US policy and actions.[67] In wrapping up the Vietnam experience, it is ironic that in a war where the main cause of frustration on the ground was getting the enemy to engage in the conventional Western sense, disengagement was the central strategic problem.

Jimmy Carter: Containment and Deterrence and Middle East Ascension

The two-year presidency of Gerald Ford added nothing to the Nixon Doctrine and involved no military interventions aside from the *Mayaguez* incident in May 1975 and a poorly planned and executed rescue operation off Cambodia that needlessly cost the lives of 41 US Marines.[68] Ford's successor did not change this trend until the Carter Doctrine was defined late in Pres. Jimmy Carter's term. It was proclaimed in his 1980 State of the Union Address and in presidential directive to the National Security Council 63 (PD/NSC-63). It responded directly to the Soviet invasion of Afghanistan in 1979 and was intended to deter Soviet attempts to expand their influence in the Persian Gulf. As Soviet troops in Afghanistan posed "a grave threat to the free movement of Middle East oil," Carter proclaimed, "An attempt by any outside force to gain control of the Persian Gulf region will be regarded as an assault on the vital interests of the United States of America, and such an assault will be repelled by any means necessary, including military force."[69]

The Carter Doctrine assumes great significance in today's context. At the time, the United States had little military presence in the Persian Gulf to support the doctrine. This, combined with the failed hostage rescue in Iran, led to the creation of the rapid deployment force, forebearer of the US Central Command. While the botched hostage rescue was a defining moment for Carter's NSS and NMS, no conflicts present themselves for the study of disengagement.

Ronald Reagan: Containment and Deterrence and Rollback of the Evil Empire

As PD/NSC-63 was not signed until January 1981, it was the launching point for Pres. Ronald Reagan's administration. Where the Carter Doctrine warned the Soviets or other outsiders from interfering in the Persian Gulf, the Reagan Corollary pledged to support internal stability, particularly that of Saudi Arabia in the context of the Iran-Iraq War. This marked the beginning of growing entanglements in Middle Eastern affairs.

Aside from the Middle East and the Reagan Corollary to the Carter Doctrine, the larger Reagan Doctrine focused on opposing the global influence of the Soviet Union. What made it different from its Cold War predecessors was its more active anti-communist approach. The Reagan Doctrine aimed not just at resisting further communist gains, but more importantly at rolling back past Soviet gains. Rollback as a national security strategy was new in practice, if not in concept. At its root, it represented a more assertive form of containment. The idea that containing Soviet aggression could not be done just at the Soviet border is seen in Korea, Vietnam, and other conflicts. However, previous presidents who had considered rolling back Soviet gains had held back for fear of the risk of nuclear escalation inherent in confronting Soviet interests so directly.[70] Thus, the strategy was certainly expansive, but the scope of Reagan's rollback strategy was broader than those of his predecessors, including much more economic and military aid than direct support and much more covert support. Rollback efforts focused on overt and covert aid to resistance movements in Africa, Asia, and Latin America.

Awkwardly straddling the two broad areas of interest in the Reagan Doctrine, Mideast engagement and Soviet rollback, is Reagan's involvement with Lebanon. It did not involve any major combat operations, but it does present an interesting minicase for disengagement.[71] The United States deployed military forces to Lebanon twice in 1982, and while the missions were different, both represent less an exit strategy and more a strategy of exit.

The first deployment from 21 August through 10 September 1982 had specific ends, achievable mainly by military means. American marines were sent along with French and Italian contingents in a multinational force tasked with overseeing the disengagement of Israeli and Palestine Liberation Organization (PLO) forces from southern Lebanon. In terms of disengagement, the arrangement worked to their favor as disengagement avoided a protracted struggle while transferring the burden to the MNF.[72] The sight picture on 10 September appeared to be a disengagement success for the United States, also. The key was Pentagon resistance to open-ended action. Secretary of Defense Caspar Weinberger was wary of nebulous State Department and National Security Council interests in leveraging the MNF for other US diplomatic actions and thus obtained a 30-day limit on the marines' deployment. This kept the mission clear. The MNF monitored and facilitated the Palestinian withdrawal and left on 10 September, when it was complete.[73]

The second deployment, barely more than a week later, was less clearly defined. Its goals were less specific and not readily achievable by military force alone. Over Weinberger's objections, a similar military means, albeit with minimal French and Italian support, was thrown at a vastly different strategic end.[74] After Lebanon's president was assassinated on 14 September and Israel entered West Beirut, the second MNF was sent in to "establish a presence."[75] The marines' mission was not clear, and their presence was seen as taking sides. When Jordan and the PLO rejected President Reagan's diplomatic initiatives in early 1982, US marines were increasingly targeted. The discord between the means and ends left the marines vulnerable and lacking the forces necessary either to stabilize Lebanon or drive Syrian-sponsored, anti-US factions out.[76]

The second MNF dragged on until 27 February 1984, with several changes in the strategic objective, from general stabilization to expulsion of Syrian forces. Through it all, the MNF's mission was not changed. What had been a great example of planned disengagement had raised expectations beyond reason. As the situation deteriorated and the United States lost all appearances of neutrality, eventually the threat morphed into a Syrian, and by association Soviet, attack on Beirut. Even after a suicide truck bomb killed 241 marines on 23 October 1983, US leaders continued to raise the stakes without doing anything to better align the military means with the strategic ends.[77]

After a massive Shia attack on Beirut in January 1984, the United States was left with the military options of withdrawing or initiating an equally massive ground offensive. Reagan chose a gradual withdrawal, but even that could not be accomplished in an orderly fashion, as the Lebanese government broke with the United States and Italy withdrew its MNF forces. Not until the marines had quickly departed by 27 February 1984 did President Reagan adopt a suitable end state, declaring the Marines could disengage, as they had accomplished their mission of averting an Israeli-Syrian war.[78] This is reminiscent of Kissinger's comment on declaring victory based on already accomplished objectives.

As noted, Secretary Weinberger and the JCS viewed the Lebanon mission as ill fated. Accordingly, they had argued against involvement in the MNF; as, in their view, the situation in Lebanon could not be solved by outside force, and any US forces committed would become a convenient and prominent target for the various factions in the civil war. The major lessons from Lebanon dovetailed with many from Vietnam. They were enunciated by Weinberger in a speech to the National Press Club in November 1984 in what became known as the Weinberger Doctrine. Its tenets included first, that US forces should be engaged only when vital national or allies' interests are at stake. Second, commit forces only wholeheartedly, with a clear intention to win. Third, commit troops to combat only with clearly defined and militarily achievable objectives. Fourth, continually reassess the mission against the forces committed. Fifth, do not commit US troops without a "reasonable assurance" of the support of US public opinion and Congress. Sixth, commit US troops only as a last resort.[79]

Before the emergence of the Weinberger Doctrine and concurrent with the second Lebanon MNF mission, President Reagan employed US forces in combat for the first time since Vietnam. Operation Urgent Fury lasted nine days, from 25 October to 3 November 1983. US forces invaded the Caribbean island of Grenada, successfully restored the popular government, rescued American citizens, and rolled back a perceived threat.[80] Much was made in the media over the mighty US military invading a tiny island to rescue medical students, but this must be viewed in the context of its proximity to the Iranian hostage crisis.

Grenada's strategic national interest to the United States lay in a socialist coup in 1979, after which the country moved closer to Cuba and the Soviet Union. In late 1983 Cuba built a runway on Grenada suitable for military aircraft and operations. An October 1983 coup by militantly anti-US marxists added to existing tensions a potential immediate threat to the nearly 600 American students and 400 other foreigners living in Grenada. Top national security advisors feared the junta might resist an evacuation and that armed Cuban construction workers might intervene. The approved objectives for the operation included rescue of the Americans, neutralization of Grenadian forces and the armed Cuban workers, and reconstruction of the Grenadian government.[81]

As the first combat operation since Vietnam, all the services insisted on being involved, despite its relatively small scale. The operation succeeded but suffered from the consequences of inadequate time for planning, lack of tactical intelligence, and problems with joint command and control. The operation accomplished its objectives but mostly by overcoming obstacles with brute force. Disengagement was smooth and prompt, said foreign affairs expert Ronald H. Cole, observing that "late in the afternoon of 2 November, after redeploying both MARG 1-84 and the *Independence* battle group to the Middle East, ADM Wesley McDonald designated MG Edward Trobaugh, 'Commander, Combined Forces, Grenada.' The combat phase of URGENT FURY had ended." Secretary Weinberger ordered Trobaugh to continue reconstruction with the goal of withdrawing all US troops as soon as the new government could stand on its own. The 82d Airborne Division reached peak strength of more than 6,000 troops in Grenada on 3 November but began redeploying almost immediately. The last battalion flew back to Fort Bragg on 12 December.[82]

Cole added that "together with the bombing of the Marine Corps barracks in Beirut that same month, the experience in Grenada added impetus to efforts to reform the joint system which were already under way."[83] Outgrowths from the lessons of Lebanon and Grenada included the Weinberger Doctrine and the Goldwater-Nichols Department of Defense Reorganization Act of 1986.[84]

Jeanne Kirkpatrick, Reagan's ambassador to the UN, may have summed it up best, saying, "President Reagan made clear that he did not intend to accept attacks on Americans passively."[85] Though hard-nosed, Reagan's foreign policy was not foolhardy. While his rollback NSS involved the United States in many conflicts during his two terms, comparatively few involved direct military intervention, and those that did tended to aim for maximum effect from minimum exposure. Learning from unwise and unnecessary exposure of ground forces in Lebanon, Reagan used overwhelming force early on in the Grenada operation to "nip the threat in the bud."

Having engaged in peacekeeping first, then an invasion for regime change, Reagan's next showdown came in response to state-sponsored terrorism. It was a long time coming; five years after his initial promise of "swift and effective retribution" to acts of terrorism.[86] Though Libyan dictator Muammar al-Qaddafi was targeted early on as the most overt state sponsor of terrorism, Reagan did not lash out militarily. Instead, the administration applied all elements of national power to pressure al-Qaddafi to change. Only when prolonged economic sanctions, diplomatic efforts, information campaigns, and even military shows of force—in the form of naval air and surface operations in contested waters off Libya—did not work, did Reagan opt for offensive military action.[87]

When the time for offensive action came, on 15 April 1986, it took the form of air strikes aimed at punishing al-Qaddafi and putting him on notice that he could not attack America or her allies with impunity.[88] Using airpower, including both Navy and Air Force assets, made disengagement inherent. Regardless of how much or how little planning is involved, airpower does not engage until the president says to engage. Once an air strike is complete, the engagement is considered complete, until or unless the president says go again. Airpower is thus uniquely advantageous for punitive engagements. Operation El Dorado Canyon was representative of a class of military engagements that are almost exclusively strategic. The mission had the limited and militarily achievable objectives of destroying critical elements of al-Qaddafi's terrorist infrastructure while minimizing American losses and Libyan civilian casualties.[89]

El Dorado Canyon did not compel al-Qaddafi to renounce terrorism completely, and it did not stop terrorism overnight. Combined with other elements of national power, as part of a unified national strategy, however, it achieved its objectives. Therefore, al-Qaddafi lost valued resources, was forced to change his methods, and was shown he was *touchable* (emphasis in original). US forces executed the strike, achieved their objectives, and disengaged, preserving their potential to fight another day in another place, as needed.

Another example of President Reagan's assertive yet *disengagement-friendly* approach arose roughly a year after Libya, in the Persian Gulf. On 7 March 1987 US Navy forces intervened in the Iran-Iraq *tanker wars*. Kuwait was caught in the middle and had asked the United States to reflag Kuwaiti tankers and provide US Navy protection. A 17 May 1987 attack by Iraqi attack aircraft using Exocet missiles against the USS *Stark* killed 37 sailors. The United States accepted Iraq's claim of pilot error, blaming Iran for hostilities in the straits. Iran generally avoided direct attacks on US escorts and minesweepers but ran continual harassment operations. When Iranian forces hit the reflagged tanker *Sea Isle City* in October 1987, the US Navy destroyed two Iranian oil platforms. The Reagan administration kept the United Nations engaged in its efforts to isolate Iran.[90] The operation involved all services but took place completely at sea. On 18 April 1988 the largest engagement of surface warships since World

War II took place as the United States eliminated a majority of Iran's navy in one day, four days after the USS *Roberts* was severely damaged by a mine. President Reagan was harshly criticized for apparently siding with Iraq, defending the interests of gulf nations that routinely purchased weapons from the Soviet Union, and for engaging US forces in an operation with no clear US interest at stake and no defined end state. Domestic pressure escalated on 3 July 1988, when the USS *Vincennes* shot down Iranian airbus A300, killing all 290 passengers.[91] President Reagan remained resolute, and ultimately the naval losses and the airbus incident helped to convince Iran to agree to a 20 August 1988 cease-fire with Iraq. Objectives accomplished, US military forces withdrew from the Persian Gulf and escorted the last tanker on 26 September 1988.[92]

The final years of Reagan's second term saw a hostile Congress, eager to criticize the Reagan Doctrine. Critics claimed it involved the United States in Third World struggles that had little to do with legitimate national interests, overextended US commitments for little if any gain, and supported unsavory dictators merely because they were not communists.[93] Partly to make NSS more public, Congress passed the Department of Defense Reorganization Act of 1986, commonly known as the Goldwater-Nichols Act.

Conclusions

This chapter examined how Cold War national security strategies related to their respective national military strategies. Relevant interventions were examined as the lenses to examine the congruence and appropriateness of the NMS to their NSS. Providing policy makers an understanding of what has and has not worked historically may inform future decisions. In sum, national security strategies in the Cold War era show remarkable continuity and evolution. Containment of Soviet communism and nuclear deterrence was the keystone to all presidents' national security strategies for over 40 years. Containment was interpreted differently by each president. It proved to be an expansive NSS, yet nuances in presidential doctrines shaped its associated national military strategies dramatically.

The strategic thinking of the superpower standoff affected all conflicts and interventions, even when the interests of capitalism versus communism scarcely could be imagined. Cold War conflicts and interventions always occurred in the shadow of a possible nuclear escalation; therefore, minor issues were more likely to be handled diplomatically or otherwise ignored. Confrontations tended to be major, similar to those in Korea, Cuba, and Vietnam—at least early on. Later, especially in the aftermath of the US debacle in Vietnam, the United States used force sparingly. When used, force usually was only loosely applied in the Cold War, superpower-rivalry context. Such conflicts as Lebanon, the Persian Gulf, and Libya had little or no roots in ideological stands against communist aggression.

In the Cold War context, certain general lessons regarding disengagement are evident. While disengagement of military forces is always desirable in terms of preserving military potential for future conflicts, it does not always fit national security objectives for a specific conflict. In some cases, like Korea, maintaining the status quo ante required a continued US presence. This is fine as long as the military is large enough to handle the burden without compromising its ability to engage in other operations. The US military ballooned from 1.5 million troops to over 3.5 million during Korea. Vietnam also saw a million-man spike to 3.5 million at its peak.[94] In the post–Vietnam, all-volunteer-force era, it would be difficult if not impossible to achieve a comparable buildup in a reasonably short period.

Aside from the extreme case where long-term engagement is beneficial and worth the cost, the next lesson is that the United States can disengage anytime it chooses, if it is willing to suffer the consequences. Disengagement under such terms is ugly, but it provides a way out of deteriorating situations. Such situations are likely to arise from poor engagement decisions or unforeseen changes in the operational environment, which render objectives unachievable. President Kennedy apparently considered such a withdrawal without a victory in Vietnam. When lost face and credibility are trumped by lost lives, it is possible to declare victory based on already accomplished objectives, as Kissinger suggested. Could such a disengagement from Vietnam between 1957 and 1967 have been any worse a calamity than the withdrawal in 1973?

The third lesson is that the force used affects disengagement. Lower-scale forms of engagement ease disengagement. Diplomacy, information, and economic/military aid do not fill body bags. When military force must be used, naval presence is a classic coercive tool that is easy to disengage. Likewise, such blockades as those that occurred during the Cuban missile crisis offer serious firepower with comparatively little risk, provided the adversary does not want the risk of escalation inherent in sinking a capital ship. Airpower options include global mobility for humanitarian relief and non-combatant evacuations and intelligence, surveillance, and reconnaissance on the non-violent end. Like maritime force, airpower can escalate from presence to full-blown air campaigns and enjoy relatively low exposure to risk and are easily turned off. The greatest complications to disengagement arise once ground troops are introduced. Therefore, from a disengagement perspective, it is best to put US ground forces in harm's way only when necessary. When ground forces are used, achievable objectives, a clear end state, and a plan for disengagement are required.

The fourth lesson, although trite, is that the easiest intervention from which to disengage forces is the one where forces were not engaged because there was no militarily achievable goal matched to the deployable force. When this concern is ignored, as in the second Lebanon MNF, disengagement is likely to be the ugly cut-and-run type.

Notes

1. Art, *Grand Strategy*.
2. Ikenberry, *After Victory*, 171.
3. Ibid., 173.
4. Brown, "Changing Circumstances of U.S. Foreign Policy," 2.
5. US Department of State, *United States Policy in the Korean Crisis: 1950*, ix.
6. Bailey, *Korean Crisis*, 5, 18. Bailey, a pacifist, Quaker, and peace researcher, takes a stance very sympathetic to communist regimes. In this particular reference, he assumes there must have been some informal discussion, but he offers no evidence.
7. US Department of State, *United States Policy in the Korean Crisis: 1950*, ix.
8. Ibid., xi.
9. Ibid.
10. Guttmann, *Korea*, 3.

11. Bailey, *Korean Crisis*, 14–15.

12. Ibid., 16.

13. US Department of State, "Resolution Adopted by the Security Council, June 25, 1950," 16.

14. US Department of State, *United States Policy in the Korean Crisis*, 2.

15. Guttmann, *Korea*, 6.

16. US Department of State, "Statement by the President," 18.

17. George, "American Policy Making," in Guttmann, ed., *Korea*, 113. Taken from *World Politics* 7 (January 1955): 209–32.

18. Ibid.

19. Dillie, *Substitute for Victory*, 19.

20. United Nations, "General Assembly Resolution of October 7, 1950," 13.

21. Guttmann, *Korea*, 21–23. MacArthur responded in a letter to House of Representatives minority leader Joseph W. Martin, and Truman posted his position in an address to the nation.

22. Horowitz, "Containment into Liberation," 114–40.

23. Bame, *Exit Strategy Myth*, 13.

24. Millis, "Truman and MacArthur," 78.

25. Dillie, *Substitute for Victory*, 11.

26. MacArthur, "Testimony before the Senate Armed Services and Foreign Relations Committees," 30–31.

27. Dillie, *Substitute for Victory*, 73.

28. Ibid., 8–10.

29. Cottrell and Dougherty, "Lessons of Korea," 175.

30. Brown, "Korea and the Balance of Power," 255.

31. Wolk, "The 'New Look'."

32. Krepinevich, *Army and Vietnam*, 17.

33. Dillie, *Substitute for Victory*, 76–78.

34. George, "American Policy-Making," 116.

35. Eliot, in introduction to Poats, *Decision in Korea*, v–x.

36. Speier, *Disengagement*, 1.

37. Krepinevich, *Army and Vietnam*, 18.

38. Kennedy, *Inaugural Address*.

39. Krepinevich, *Army and Vietnam*, 27.

40. Allison and Zelikow, *Essence of Decision*, 89.

41. Ibid., 111–20.

42. Ibid., 129.

43. Krepinevich, *Army and Vietnam*, 29.

44. Ibid., 29–36.

45. Ibid., 33–34.

46. Logevall, *Choosing War*, 375.

47. Ibid., xiii.

48. Ibid., xvii. The conventional wisdom here was established by Gelb and Betts, *Irony of Vietnam*, 244.

49. Galbraith, "Exit Strategy." Dr. James K. Galbraith, a 2003 Carnegie scholar, holds the Lloyd M. Bentsen Jr. Chair of Government/Business Relations at the Lyndon B. Johnson School of Public Affairs, University of Texas

at Austin. His father, Kenneth Galbraith, was Pres. John F. Kennedy's ambassador to Vietnam and advocated US withdrawal from Vietnam as early as April 1962.

50. Ibid.

51. Ibid.

52. Krepinevich, *Army and Vietnam*, 258.

53. Ibid., 249. The number is at the extreme high end and is drawn from Oberdorfer, *Tet!*, 295.

54. Pribbenow, *Victory in Vietnam*, 231. See also Dougan and Weiss, *Vietnam Experience*.

55. Krepinevich, *Army and Vietnam*, 250.

56. Oberdorfer, *Tet!*, 295.

57. Karnow, *Vietnam*, 581.

58. Worden, *Rise of the Fighter Generals*, 194.

59. Karnow, *Vietnam*, 597.

60. Ibid., 604.

61. Ibid., 608–9.

62. US Department of Defense, "Melvin R. Laird."

63. Karnow, *Vietnam*, 602.

64. US Department of Defense, "Melvin R. Laird."

65. Laird, "Iraq: Learning the Lessons."

66. Kissinger, *Diplomacy*, 700–701.

67. Bame, *Exit Strategy Myth*, 14.

68. US Maritime Service Veterans, "Capture and Release of SS *Mayaguez*."

69. Carter, *Presidential Directive/NSC-63*.

70. Bodenheimer and Gould, *Rollback!*

71. Bame, *Exit Strategy Myth*. Bame uses Lebanon as a case study for the two euphemistic elements of disengagement, end state and exit strategy. See also Hallenbeck, *Military Force*; and Martin and Walcott, *Best Laid Plans*.

72. Bame, *Exit Strategy Myth*, 16; and Hallenbeck, *Military Force*, 28–30.

73. Martin and Walcott, *Best Laid Plans*, 93–94.

74. Bame, *Exit Strategy Myth*, 18.

75. Hammel, *Root*, 38.

76. Bame, *Exit Strategy Myth*, 19–20.

77. Hammel, *Root*, 38, 217–21; and Hallenbeck, *Military Force*, 81–84.

78. Hallenbeck, *Military Force*, 123–27.

79. Weinberger, "Uses of Military Power."

80. Cole, *Operation Urgent Fury*, 1.

81. Ibid., 2.

82. Ibid., 61–62.

83. Ibid., 2.

84. Ibid., 7.

85. Kirkpatrick, "U.S. National Security Strategy."

86. Stanik, *El Dorado Canyon*, ix.

87. Ibid., xi–xii.

88. Ibid., xii.

89. Ibid., 147.

90. GlobalSecurity.org, "Operation Earnest Will."
91. Koppel, "USS *Vincennes*."
92. Peniston, *No Higher Honor.*
93. Carpenter, "U.S. Aid to Anti-Communist Rebels."
94. Yost, "Future of U.S. Overseas Presence," 73.

Chapter 4

Disengagement in the New World Order

The political leadership is unlikely to make change any more attractive now in terms of additional resources than was the case under the Kennedy and Johnson administrations. The ends-means disconnect that existed during the days of the "two-and-a-half-war" strategy, in the early 1960s, exists today.

—Andrew Krepinevich
The Army and Vietnam

The Goldwater-Nichols Act requires the president to submit to Congress an annual report outlining the NSS that he or she will pursue while in office.[1] Having a legal requirement for a commander in chief to publish the nation's grand strategy for public and legislative oversight may be uniquely American. This reporting requirement, an amendment to the Goldwater-Nichols Act, gave Congress some control, a baseline for judgment, and conferred accountability for strategic planning on the executive branch. In 1994 Senator Strom Thurmond noted a trend that continues 20 years after the passage of Goldwater-Nichols: presidential compliance with reporting requirements has "seldom met the expectations of those of us who participated in passing the Goldwater-Nichols Act."[2] Complaints generally center on lack of timeliness and vagueness. Such *you can make me write it, but you can't make me say anything* power struggles between the executive and legislative branches cannot be helpful.

Goldwater-Nichols aimed at improving military efficiency and strategic planning, establishing command relationships, ensuring JCS authority, and avoiding executive micromanagement in the shadow of Vietnam, Iran, Lebanon, and Grenada. The reforms focused on the internal dynamics of the president, the secretary of defense (SECDEF), and the joint chiefs.[3] Not only must the president provide the NSS to the SECDEF and the

JCS, he also has to confer with them in its drafting. Such reporting requirement should ensure that the NMS matches the NSS. More specifically, the NSS is required to include a comprehensive description and discussion of the following concerns:

1. The worldwide interests, goals, and objectives of the United States that are vital to the national security of the United States

2. The foreign policy, worldwide commitments, and national defense capabilities of the United States necessary to deter aggression and to implement the national security strategy of the United States

3. The proposed short-term and long-term uses of the political, economic, military, and other elements of the national power of the United States to protect or promote the interests and achieve the goals and objectives referred to in (1)

4. The adequacy of the capabilities of the United States to carry out the national security strategy of the United States, including an evaluation of the balance among the capabilities of all elements of the national power of the United States to support the implementation of the national security strategy.[4]

Goldwater-Nichols sought to remedy several military strategic planning deficiencies outlined in the Locher report. The critical problems, according to Locher, lay in the Department of Defense's planning, programming, and budgeting system (PPBS). Introduced by SECDEF Robert S. McNamara, PPBS is "the formal process for arriving at resource allocation decisions. Its purpose is the translation of military strategy and planning into specific defense programs and the development of defense programs into a budget request."[5] James Locher argues that planning was the weak link, quoting former undersecretary of defense Robert W. Komer who said that "there is all too little systematic strategy making in DOD, except in the strategic nuclear arena. Instead the reality is best characterized as a piecemeal, irregular, highly informal process, largely driven by cumulative program decisions influenced more by budget constraints and consequent inter-service competition than by notions of US strategic priorities."[6]

Under Goldwater-Nichols, the NSS process begins with the president. Once the NSS is complete, the SECDEF adds a report detailing budget planning and procurement for the programs affected by the NSS and justifies any military missions to be conducted pursuant to the NSS. At this point, the chairman of the Joint Chiefs of Staff submits a study outlining the direction of the NMS for strategic and contingency planning.[7] In theory, Congress saw Goldwater-Nichols as fixing historical strategic planning blunders by formally connecting desired ends (NSS) to ways (NMS) through stable means (resource allocation).[8]

President Reagan reiterated the importance of the process in his first NSS report, saying, "To be effective, it must be firmly rooted in broad national interests and objectives, supported by national resources, and integrate all relevant facets of national power to achieve our national objectives."[9] The first formal NSS report under Goldwater-Nichols, President Reagan's, is indicative of what most post–World War II NSSs would reflect. Written in the context of the Cold War, it focused on the then 40-year standoff with the Soviet Union and continued the basic foreign policy prescription of containment (ch. 2, table 2).

Likewise, Reagan's defense prescription on deterrence is a continuance of basic Cold War doctrine.[10] Note that deterrence had many flavors through the years. Reagan's defense policy featured international engagement through alliances over an arms race mentality.[11] As noted earlier, the Reagan Doctrine, echoed in his NSS, added rollback to the long-standing Truman Doctrine. Few anticipated the success of the strategy.

Post–Cold War—Engagement and Enlargement

In the immediate post-Reagan years, three presidents advanced polices in response to the Cold War. Beginning with former vice president George H. W. Bush, each president had the opportunity to view the post–Cold War era differently.

George H. W. Bush: Multilateral Engagement in the New World Order

George H. W. Bush presided over the fall of the Soviet Union and the first fundamental shift in the bipolar international order. Published after the 1991 Gulf War, his NSS focused on the new world order: "If there is a coherent focus in the report, it is in the emphasis on America's role as an alliance leader in the international community."[12] Largely a rundown of geopolitical changes, it does show the first signs of emerging missions in light of the Soviet Union's demise. The report adds illicit drugs and crisis response to more traditional topics of disarmament, weapons proliferation, force deployments, and military restructuring.[13] This first foray into post–Cold War NSS was no slam dunk. Bush's NSS was opposed by both Republicans and Dememocrats. Conservatives saw multilateralism as suborning US national interests to the United Nations. Liberals saw it as too focused on military instruments of power and traditional hard-power aspects of national security.[14]

If multilateral engagement is the theme of the NSS, the NMS might best be characterized as deter and defeat. Faced with an opportunity to rethink military requirements in the absence of the Soviet bear, the NMS was built around a smaller *base force* concept tasked to decisively win two major regional contingencies concurrently.

Not particularly coherent as a national strategy, Bush's NSS did shine light on the uncertainty of the post–Cold War era and his perception of the growing importance of the global economy. At least one author sees hints of preemption in George H. W. Bush's crisis-response philosophy: "A key task for the future will be maintaining regional balances and resolving such disputes before they erupt into military conflict."[15]

Operation Just Cause in Panama in December 1989 might best be characterized as a preventive operation. While still within the Cold War context of containment, it marks a tipping point into a more global economic motivation for conflict vice the ideological standard of previous decades. The United States undertook the operation to capture Gen Manuel Noriega, commander of the Panamanian Defense Force, a brutal drug trafficker and the real power in Panama. His efforts to consolidate power included repression of civil liberties and assaults on US military personnel.[16]

Fighting a limited war, close to home and against an adversary without neighboring superpower backing, led to rapid military success. Disengagement was not anticipated to be a major problem, as the government already was in place to take over when Noriega was removed. Also, Panama was unique in that the United States had a long-standing presence in-country. Still, despite some complications from overly sequential operations, planners recognized that success relied on more than just military forces, and they "tried to determine . . . what the end of the war should look like (and) work backwards."[17] Consistent with military culture, however, planners focused linearly, and therefore exclusively, on decisive military operations. Unfortunately, a different team was planning post-combat operations; so, the combat planners were not starting from the right target.[18]

President Bush's NSS called for multilateral engagement. Yet, his specific desired end state in this operation was for the US military to unilaterally "create an environment safe for Americans [in Panama], ensure the integrity of the Panama Canal, provide a stable environment for the freely elected Endara government, and bring Noriega to justice."[19] Bush's NMS of deter and defeat was consistent with this task. The NMS didn't explicitly include language regarding civil affairs tasks such as garbage collection and law enforcement. Still, US ground forces arrived in sufficient numbers to successfully, if somewhat awkwardly, manage to quell rampant lawlessness and looting.[20]

Order was reestablished quickly, but it was not restored before public opinion was tainted. Though post-conflict operations (PCO) planners expected looting as the established military structure of order collapsed, security barriers between the DOD and the Department of State had hindered detailed planning. Gen Frederick Frank Woerner, commander, US Southern Command, said the DOD was "planning an invasion of a friendly nation with whom we have diplomatic relations from bases internal to that country. Pretty sensitive issue, especially when you've got base negotiations going on in the Philippines."[21] Organizational structure is not alone to blame. Warrior culture is visible in that Gen Maxwell Thurman, the incoming US Southern Command commander, "did not even spend five minutes" on PCO plans during his inbriefing to the command.[22]

If Operation Just Cause were a tentative step beyond Cold War superpower rivalry, Desert Storm was the full operational test of post–Vietnam US military transformation and the Reagan buildup. In line with the NSS and the NMS, Desert Storm engaged a multilateral coalition to deter and then defeat Saddam Hussein's annexation of Kuwait.

As the North Atlantic Treaty Organization and the Warsaw Pact had represented the bipolar collective security paradigm of the Cold War, in 1990 Pres George H. W. Bush sought to align good against evil in the new world order proclaimed in his NSS. To achieve the desired transformation, the Bush administration accepted end-state limitations required by its Gulf Cooperation Council and other coalition partners. Ultimately, the moderating tendencies of these agreements eased US strategic military disengagement. In turn, this pattern enabled such non-military policy tools as political and economic sanctions to yield further benefits to US interests.

In a larger version of the first Lebanon MNF and demonstrating lessons learned from the second, US military forces were used for specific purposes. The realistic limits imposed by the coalition, coupled with the Weinberger/Powell Doctrine, successfully resisted the tendencies toward overreach and expansion of missions.

The most important limitation, from either a positive or a negative perspective, was that which precluded regime change as an objective of the campaign. Dictators like Saddam Hussein, leading repressive and exclusionary regimes, often survive all but the most disastrous of defeats. Because of this, they are prone to settle when it is clear they will lose.[23] Whether US leaders believed Saddam could survive defeat, the use of force for regime change was undesirable for coalition cohesion. According to Pres. George H. W. Bush in an 8 August speech to the nation, the resultant desired military end state was thus clear: "First, we seek the immediate, unconditional, and complete withdrawal of all Iraqi forces from Kuwait. Second, Kuwait's legitimate government must be restored."[24]

The result was the seemingly straightforward decision by President Bush to disengage military forces, once these criteria were met. Still, the decision to disengage had to be made by the president. On the surface, the situation had many parallels to Korea: similar objectives and the ability (indeed the temptation) to press forward once the original objectives were met. Therefore, the decision was not so straightforward. Nowhere in the NSS or NMS was a clear indication that military disengagement would occur at some specific time or in some specific way after achievement of an end state. Though there was no set time line as there had been with the first Lebanon MNF, the outcome of Desert Storm was similar. Clear, finite, achievable military objectives, coupled with restraint of mission creep, led to a mission clearly accomplished and an orderly disengagement to allow other instruments of power back to the fore. Desert Storm seems the perfect case for proper disengagement.

Critics, however, continue to this day to second-guess Pres. G. H. W. Bush's decision to disengage when he did, based on the facts that Saddam's regime did not fall and his elite Republican Guard units were not destroyed. Bush's critics almost immediately began using these facts, along with veiled statements of support to anti-Saddam groups and overrestrictive cease-fire conditions, to weaken public perception of victory.

It has been said that nothing fails like success. When, again like Lebanon, US forces were called in to engage in subsequent operations, the objectives expanded beyond those the military reasonably could attain. While Saddam's overthrow might have been attainable by military means, the alternative of his full acceptance of UN Security Council resolutions was not.[25] Without criteria for mission achievement, disengagement cannot come as an orderly step in a process.

Lebanon and Desert Storm suggest failure to remain disengaged can have varied consequences. In Lebanon, overly ambitious objectives for the second MNF led to mission creep and eventual disaster. In Iraq, failure to engage the proper personnel and the correct instruments of national power led to an incomplete cease-fire arrangement, which in turn resulted in the nearly immediate engagement of US forces in new missions. No-fly-zone (NFZ) enforcement missions lacked an attainable end state. The resulting open-ended missions led not to lost lives but to a lengthy deployment, continuing mission creep, and a costly drain on US Air Force personnel and equipment.[26] Air exclusion zones, or NFZ enforcement, represent opportunities for airpower to offer strategic advantage, but the missions can be abused in the absence of attainable objectives. Failure to disengage from the frustrating, open-ended missions in a reasonable time arguably led to Operation Iraqi Freedom and contributed to the recapitalization quandary the Air Force faces today.

If Desert Storm had similarities to the first Lebanon MNF in terms of congruence between ends and means, Somalia looked more like the second MNF. Like Lebanon 10 years earlier, the US intervention in Somalia fell into two separate phases. The first was a limited humanitarian relief mission, from August to November 1992. The military focused on securing delivery points and access for relief supplies. President Bush set military objectives appropriate for the force, while the State Department worked with the United Nations on broader objectives, including additional means to ensure delivery of relief.[27]

The United Nations initiated the humanitarian relief program, yet failed to enforce its authorizations. Only 500 of 3,000 authorized UN troops were deployed. This proved insufficient for security or stability; so, eventually the United States agreed to reinforce the mission.[28] The second deployment was a United States–led multinational united task force (UNITAF) that included 28,000 Americans. What it had in size, it lacked in specific, militarily achievable objectives. Tasked "to establish a secure environment for humanitarian relief operations" for a follow-on UN force likely to be deployed in late January 1993, the mission was an interim fix with no achievable end state.[29] Smith Hempstone, the US ambassador to Kenya, noted this problematic US policy and told a US news magazine, "If you liked Beirut, you'll love Somalia."[30]

By mid-December, the worst of the famine was past, but US policy objectives continued to escalate.[31] Delivering relief was no longer sufficient to warrant disengagement of military forces. Assistant secretary of state Herman Cohen set the bar higher on 17 December 1992, saying, "All our good works could go for naught if we do not follow through on the long and difficult process of reconstituting Somalia's civil society and government."[32]

This is how incongruences emerge and quagmires begin. State Department diplomats are eager to leverage military forces. For this to work, the threat of military intervention has to be coordinated with the DOD, and the use of military force has to be feasible. If adversaries call diplomats' bluffs, it is not the State Department that is left suspended in midair. As we are reminded so often, the State Department does not have the personnel and equipment to carry out the nation-building and peacekeeping operations they champion.

This was the case in Somalia. Diplomats implied threats to Somali warlords that were nowhere in the military mission, which was aimed at securing the environment for humanitarian efforts with minimal use of force in the shortest time. President

Bush specifically wanted to turn over "the stability mission to the follow-on United Nations Mission in Somalia (UNOSOM) because (1) the mission appeared well within the capabilities of such a force, and (2) President Bush had no wish to saddle the incoming Clinton administration with such a deployment of US forces."[33] Unfortunately, turnover to the weaker UN-led force did not constitute a sufficient strategy for disengagement. Disengagement was not complete, as SECDEF Dick Cheney and JCS chief, Gen Colin Powell, had to promise US forces to support UNOSOM should the need arise.[34]

Bill Clinton: Engagement and Enlargement

Pres. George H. W. Bush's acceptance of the Somalia mission officially added humanitarian intervention to the realm of US foreign policy. His successor, Bill Clinton, continued this expansion of the national security domain. Clinton's worldview of "constructive engagement," coupled with Secretary of State Madeleine Albright's "assertive multilateralism," ensured the 1990s would be filled with a variety of military interventions, including Somalia, Bosnia, Haiti, and Kosovo.[35] As an enunciated strategy, President Clinton's NSS of engagement and enlargement is perhaps the most readily identifiable target when looking for a point where military disengagement became materially hindered by an unnatural congruence between NSS and NMS.

Despite President Bush's intention of wrapping up operations in Somalia before leaving office, the Clinton administration had to deal with a continued US presence. The UNITAF-to-UNOSOM mission transfer did not occur until May 1993. President Clinton did not change policy and thus faced the prospect of having Americans as part of a less-capable force with a poorly defined mission. As the administrations changed, Clinton had the opportunity to change policy in one of two ways. He could disengage in the literal sense of breaking Bush's commitment to UNOSOM, or he could escalate. To the Clinton administration's credit, it did not escalate, even declining requests for more specially trained US forces, along with tanks and armored vehicles. By choosing the status quo over disengagement, and in fact expanding the already dubious mission to one of nation building, Clinton was accountable for not expanding the US force when 18 US soldiers were killed in October 1993. Blame was laid on SECDEF Les Aspin for denying requested troops and weapons. Aspin was fired, and only then did the administration decide, much like the second MNF in Lebanon 10 years earlier, to disengage by March 1994.[36] Unlike Lebanon, President Clinton could not even rationalize a victory. The best opportunity for that passed in late 1992, when the worst of the famine was past and the original military mission ballooned.

Blame for the quagmire and policy debacle of Somalia is not important. There is plenty to go around between the Bush and the Clinton administrations. Both had opportunities to disengage somewhat gracefully from a situation at least some foresaw. Neither Bush nor Clinton adequately considered strategic military disengagement as an enabler for other instruments of national power, and neither embraced an exit strategy. As in Lebanon, the United States relied on military *presence* to support diplomatic options. Again, presence only increased opposition to US forces and blocked both the diplomatic and military efforts.[37]

President Clinton's own NSS is better defined apart from the inherited Somalian intervention. More so than his predecessors, Clinton seemed to grasp the gravitas of putting his name to strategic doctrine for the nation. This shows in its explicit naming. Yet, his NSS still grasped at the same uncertainties of the post–Cold War world as did its predecessor.[38] Lacking the focusing agent of the Cold War, Clinton chose a broad, liberal, internationalist conception of US interests. To President Bush's additions of illicit drugs and transnational terrorism, President Clinton added "commercial goals and the spread of liberal-democratic ideals into the group of fundamental national interests."[39] That Clinton was still struggling with a replacement for containment is echoed by John Lewis Gaddis's assessment that "there was the sense (in the administration) that the war had been won, the fundamental processes in world politics (globalization and self-determination) were favorable to us, and therefore you could just kind of sit back and let them run."[40]

Idealistic, perhaps, and certainly expansive, Clinton's vision was not unattainable; however, it became overly expansive and unrealistic when combined with the other ideal Clinton sought—the peace dividend. Drastically shrinking defense spending while concurrently expanding military roles and missions does not make sense. Compounding the problem were the other instruments of national security that were being cut also. Defense cuts would make sense, if the cuts were applied toward building up the other instruments of power to levels necessary to accomplish the nation-building and peacekeeping missions Clinton's NSS foretold. Expanding the NSS while cutting the funds to support it, however, was overreach waiting to happen.

The imperative of engagement pointed to America's role as a global economic and political leader, enlarging democracy and free markets around the world. This global imperative and expansive conception of US interests naturally led to an equally expansive list of threats to US interests. Where the bipolar Cold War world had demanded the preponderance of attention be dedicated to global thermonuclear war and the balance of power between capitalism and communism, the new world order reweighted national security toward five threat areas. First were regional states with the capabilities and intent to threaten US vital interests. Examples include the later-named *axis of evil*—Iran, Iraq, and North Korea. Second were transnational threats like terrorism, international crime, drug trafficking, uncontrolled refugee migrations, and environmental damage. Third was the proliferation of weapons of mass destruction (WMD). Fourth was the threat posed by foreign intelligence collection. Fifth were the failed states.[41]

The reality that sprang from President Clinton's rhetoric proved to be an enormous burden on the US military in terms of foreign interventions related to the expansive expectations of the NSS.[42] When the nation is *interested* in nearly everything, it must answer threats nearly everywhere and all the time. No one engages in the threat-response business more than the military. *While President Clinton's strategy aimed to integrate all elements of national power, in reality the military element ended up taking on several "nontraditional" missions to cover for structural problems in other areas.* While on one hand cutting defense budgets to recognize the post–Cold War "peace dividend," Clinton's strategy maintained the status quo of a substantial overseas presence against the more traditional regional or state-centered threats while nurturing diplomacy and international alliances and organizations. By emphasizing multilateral commitments and forward presence, the strategy aimed to deter potential regional aggressors.

The strategy strained the system in its non-traditional focal points. *Broad additions of nebulous threats posed by transnational actors, WMD, and failed states levied great expectations on a national security apparatus ill prepared to live up to them.* While the Clinton concept of engagement is straightforward and proactive for all elements of national power, its impact on the military was underestimated. True, the demise of the bipolar superpower standoff did not do away with the need for the United States to remain engaged internationally. Clinton's 2000 NSS preempted any thought of isolation, pointing out that "the inexorable trend of globalization supports the continued viability of a strategy of engagement."[43] Rationalizing a huge cut in defense spending to pay for domestic social programs within this framework, however, was ideological folly. Again, the only reasonable place to apply the dividend was toward a revamped national security apparatus more attuned to the new world order.

Likewise, the second part of the NSS, enlargement, was logical and well intentioned but added indirect burdens to the military. Referring most directly to the enlargement of the North Atlantic Treaty Organization, "the world's most successful security organization," it also reflected on the globalization of democracy through trade.[44] Again, Clinton proposed lofty, idealistic goals that would make demands on the military. Even without exporting democracy, adding less-capable, less-stable countries to collective security agreements ensured an even greater role for the US military if those agreements were ever called into play.

President Clinton's prescriptions for NSS had serious implications for the NMS. First, in endorsing engagement, President Clinton warned, "We must not, in reaction to the real or perceived costs of engagement, retreat into a policy of 'Fortress America.'"[45] This statement introduces confusion into what is otherwise a clearly internationalist foreign policy. Nothing in previous doctrines, all of which stressed active partnerships and alliances, pointed to an isolationist Fortress America undercurrent. From the military standpoint, however, the strategy seems to preclude any thought of disengaging military forces from Cold War forward bases.

Second, and perhaps the most significant nuance of President Clinton's NSS for the NMS, is the distinction he makes between types of national interests. National interests are categorized as vital, important, and humanitarian, where categories determine the level of engagement that may be necessary.[46] Coupled with the perception that globalization necessarily binds American influence to other nations' policies, this arguably opened the door to new and varied military missions.[47] Such expansive interests and global influence combined with Secretary of State Madeleine Albright's affinity for using military forces in support of essentially diplomatic efforts, reminiscent of the 1930s' characterization of the US Marines as "State Department Forces."[48] Clinton's NMS thus represented a move toward assertive multilateral engagement and collective security.

In the DOD, seeking greater payoff from the *peace dividend,* SECDEF Les Aspin pushed a bottom-up review (BUR) of military forces. As senator, Aspin had been thwarted by the Bush administration in similar efforts. Under the resultant BUR cuts, the major regional contingency construct was revised from decisively winning two conflicts concurrently to focusing on one while holding a second stable and then turning to the second conflict once the first was resolved. This NMS became known as Win-Hold-Win. Though Aspin did not survive Somalia, his force-structure changes did. The structure was put to a test in 1994, and it quickly became clear that the United States did not have the forces necessary to deal concurrently with two potential major theater wars. Saddam Hussein moved forces south to threaten Kuwait, just as the United States was withdrawing forces and posturing for a potential conflict with North Korea.[49]

So by 1994, there already were apparent disconnects between the expansive NSS of engagement and enlargement and the NMS aimed at reducing force structure and capabilities to capture a peace dividend, without concurrent restructuring of the instruments of power better suited to support disengagement. Yet, these disconnects did not always present themselves as incongruence between the NSS and the NMS.

71

A shining example of how military action can indeed gain a sustainable advantage or better state of peace is the US intervention in Haiti in 1994. Though national security objectives shifted throughout the operation, they never moved outside the bounds of the national military strategic means. Selective engagement and collective security worked, as US intervention reduced threats to US interests and facilitated a successful transition to a UN force. In one sense, Haiti represents exactly the type of concept for which disengagement strives. It took three years of diplomatic and economic sanctions before military action was taken. Once military force was used, the objective was to do what was necessary to transition the situation back to other instruments of power, as exercised by the United Nations.[50]

At first glance, Haiti had structures similar to those found in Somalia. It was a limited mission in a failed state with primarily humanitarian objectives worked in conjunction with the United Nations. More significant were the differences; many of them are too detailed to treat here. The key was that the United States had not deployed forces to Haiti as it had in Somalia. When the United States and Canada sent military police and engineers to establish training operations according to the United Nations mission in Haiti (UNMIH), armed militias prevented their ship from docking. Unlike Lebanon and Somalia, when the troops deploying to Haiti faced threats beyond the scope of the mission, namely to land safely in a permissive environment, decision makers paused to reassess the situation. To be fair, context matters here, as the Black Hawk incident in Somalia occurred the week before the Haitian landing.[51] Regardless of cause, the fact remains that *disengagement in this case was actually restraint from engagement.* Instead of escalating tensions by putting US troops in harm's way, the Clinton administration returned to economic and diplomatic pressure.

By late summer of 1994, a military strategy including both permissive and non-permissive options was worked out, consistent with the national security ends and including feasible plans for disengagement of US forces when the ends were met. UN Security Council Resolution 940 authorized a 6,000-troop multinational force for six months that was followed by a new UNMIH to assume the diplomatic tasks.[52] *The success of this operation supports the proposition that military disengagement after attainment of realistic military goals facilitates the attainment of other national security ends.*

Of course, the assumption is that other instruments of power have the means necessary to meet their ends. Engagement and enlargement placed enormous demands on the military instrument, while reducing its means in the name of a peace dividend. President Clinton's NSS, along with Madeleine Albright's affinity for military peace-and-stability operations, led to US military involvement in Bosnia in 1995 and again in Kosovo in 1999. Whereas Operation Just Cause in Panama in 1989 was a step away from the standard Cold War intervention, the collapse of Yugoslavia was an early casualty of the end of the Cold War. Twelve years after the Bosnian intervention, long-term success remains elusive. There is peace in Bosnia and Kosovo because of strong military forces deployed there, but the ethnic tensions that spawned fratricidal warfare remain, and the pluralistic democracy the international community wishes to establish is still a dream. While it took more than 10 years to disengage US military forces, for much of that time Bosnia and Kosovo were anonymous operations with small footprints and virtually no casualties. Some observers might argue that disengagement is not important, provided operations can be kept small and relatively low key. With the unlimited resources available, this might be true, but the cumulative effect of small contingencies lasts for decades and makes a policy of disengagement important. The current US military force structure cannot support long-term engagement in many locales if the services are to be prepared for major combat operations.[53]

In Bosnia by July 1995, the desired political end state under Clinton's NSS was "a peaceful resolution to the ethnic crisis and a democratically elected, multiethnic government for Bosnia-Herzegovina, free to exercise all instruments of power within its internationally recognized borders."[54] The supporting military strategy included neutralizing threats and taking "away what the Bosnian Serbs held dear" to "drive them to military parity with the Bosnian Croats and Muslims."[55] Disengagement under these terms requires an enforceable peace treaty.

One aspect of US involvement in Bosnia is particularly interesting in terms of disengagement. Like Desert Storm, Bosnia was a coalition operation. This had particular bearing because the British and French held a different view than the United States on the nature of the conflict, resulting in a markedly different way of prosecuting operations that ultimately impacted disengagement. The United States viewed the Bosnian crisis as primarily caused by Serbian aggression and expansionism. In this aggressor-victim view, intervention or aid to the Bosnian government against the Serbs is prescribed.[56] Clinton followed this approach to avoid direct military engagement beyond NATO and UN-sanctioned NFZ enforcement in Operation Deny Flight. Minimal engagement, and particular emphasis on air, vice ground engagement, eases disengagement. *Note, again, airpower's inherent advantages as a key, and sometimes sole, military component to an NMS of rational or selective engagement. This is doubly so in an NMS of disengagement.*

America's NATO and UN partners, particularly Britain and France, viewed Bosnia as a civil war. Their view favors impartial peacekeeping or peace enforcement over taking sides.[57] Such impartiality reined in the potential for a more aggressive US military intervention, often to the chagrin of US planners. While it may have kept the United States from alienating a faction by taking sides, one may also argue that peacekeeping requires a ground-force presence that is more easily goaded into undesired escalations, which complicate disengagement.

Two things stand out in the Bosnia and Kosovo campaigns. Both were air campaigns, yet neither engaged US nor allied ground forces. The ultimate success of the Bosnian campaign in Operation Deliberate Force benefited from, if not relied on, the actions of indigenous ground forces. In Kosovo, Operation Allied Force was trumpeted widely as a case of airpower deciding the conflict.

Clinton was criticized in both operations for refusing to commit ground forces. While the cleverness of announcing the strategy publicly is open for debate, the decision not to use ground troops was sound from the standpoint of disengagement. The benefits of ground forces for the campaigns were debatable, and any military objectives would be difficult to attain. But, it is clear that the limited objectives were achievable using only airpower. Air strikes offer the clear advantage of easy disengagement because leaders can turn airpower on and off like a spigot. Finally, with limited goals, airpower reduced the risk of body bags fracturing an already tenuous alliance, re-peating Somalia or empowering Slobodan Milosevic at the bar-gaining table in an operation dependent on a peace settlement.[58] Still, it cannot be denied that the accomplishments were less than satisfying. The war was "as a deliberate act of policy, a perfect failure"[59] It did not halt ethnic cleansing or settle sover-eignty questions. It did not meet humanitarian goals, and the people of the Balkans did not see their lives tangibly improve. But, the United States disengaged, and to the American public, the mission was a success. In Iraq and Afghanistan, US forces stayed after meeting the primary objectives, and the American public largely perceived a losing effort.

As if the Balkans, Caribbean, and Horn of Africa were not enough to test Aspin's theory that the country was unlikely to face multiple military contingencies simultaneously, other state and non-state actors kept the 1990s interesting. Throughout the decade, Saddam Hussein kept Iraq in the international limelight, and non-state terrorists continued to emerge. After learning in 1994 that the United States could not afford to de-ploy massive numbers of troops every time Saddam acted pro-vocatively, Clinton increasingly relied on *cruise missile diplo-macy* to deal with both Saddam and terrorists. In August 1996, when Hussein mirrored his 1994 gambit with a similar move-ment north, Clinton responded with a cruise missile attack. In a shocking exaggeration of the sanitary, low-risk nature of pre-cision air strikes and demonstrating a flagrant discordance be-tween policy ends and military means, the cruise missiles tar-geted antiaircraft sites in the south. The 1996 strike was clearly an example of striking what was within reach vice what was relevant to the fight at hand.

This abuse of airpower's inherent advantages in terms of dis-engagement showed that air forces are not immune to being mired in situations where the means or rules of engagement do not match the desired NSS ends. American policy makers faced options similar to those in Lebanon, Somalia, and Haiti. They could disengage air forces on the one hand, release restraints on airpower to make the means better match the desired ends on the other, or take some middle path. By taking the middle ground of the status quo, supplemented with a handful of largely symbolic cruise missile strikes, the credibility of the

United States' coercive ability was weakened. More importantly, Clinton's commitment was challenged, and Saddam was emboldened not only to further repress the Kurds in the north but also to resist sanctions and regimes of inspections.

The rise of non-state terrorist groups like al-Qaeda also escalated in the 1990s. Terrorism was not new. Terrorists bombed the Marine barracks in Beirut in 1983, and Libyan-backed terrorists' actions led to Operation El Dorado Canyon. Whether due to US ties to Israel, regional resentment over the two-decade-old focus of US interest in the oil-rich region, or just merely because the large US presence created targets of opportunity, these episodes of non-state-sponsored terrorism demonstrated that disengagement is contingent on a cooperative adversary. Yet, there is no unilateral disengagement from terrorism. On Clinton's watch bombings occurred at the World Trade Center in New York City; Khobar Towers in Riyadh, Saudi Arabia; US embassies in Tanzania and Kenya; and on the USS *Cole* in Yemen.[60]

George W. Bush: Aggressive Unilateralism and Preemption

The terrorist attacks of 11 September 2001 defined the presidency of George W. Bush. Before this reality changed the national agenda, presidential candidate George W. Bush promised a more humble foreign policy. Before 9/11, the Bush strategy appeared focused on aggressive non-multilateralism. He strongly opposed Clinton-era peacekeeping and nation-building efforts. "The purpose of the military," Bush argued, "was to fight and win the nation's wars, not to linger to bring stability to newly ordained states."[61] Bush's focus was much more tightly centered on direct US national interests.

Post-9/11 events, however, forced the administration to shift its focus. The new emphasis on unilateralism and offensive use of force, while controversial, focused the NSS on a defined, if not clearly identifiable, threat.[62] Conservatives applauded the 2002 NSS as marking, in the words of Charles Krauthammer, "a return to the unabashed unilateralism of the 1980s. . . . The 1980s model went by the name of peace through strength. But it was more than that. It was judicious but unapologetic unilateralism. It was willingness—in the face of threats and bluster from foreign adversaries and nervous apprehension from domestic critics—to do what the U.S. needed to do for its own security. Regardless."[63]

Pres. George W. Bush's 2002 NSS is particularly significant, as it marks a dramatic shift from previous administrations' views of containment and deterrence. The attacks of 9/11 showed containment and deterrence to be ineffective strategies against the threat of terrorism. President Bush's lesson seems to be that a policy of preemption may have prevented the attacks; thus, "as a matter of common sense and self-defense, America will act against such emerging threats before they are fully formed."[64]

President Bush's prescriptions are direct and preemptive, diverging from previous notions of uncertainty and placing terrorism as the currently defining phenomenon and enemy. Where Pres. George H. W. Bush and President Clinton were passive, focusing on a "we must" ideology, Pres. George W. Bush's NSS is aggressive and specific and focuses on a "we will" view.[65] As well as pointing to a fundamental shift in NSS, Bush's NSS also adds a strong moral element, reflecting "the union of our values and our national interests."[66] A strong streak of American exceptionalism rang out in its tone. Understandable in the context of its timing after 9/11, such emotional language nonetheless must have implications for implementation. NMS has few options open, given such statements in the NSS as "in the new world we have entered, the only path to peace and security is the path of action."[67] The ongoing global war on terror both shaped the 2002 NSS and is shaped by it. The US military has not disengaged from Afghanistan and Iraq. The problem, as we're still involved, is that the military is too close to focus and too committed to disengage rationally.

Conclusions

This chapter examined how national security strategies since the end of the Cold War related to their concurrent national military strategies. As with chapter 2, relevant conflicts served as the lenses to examine the congruence and appropriateness of the NMSs to their NSSs. Since the end of the Cold War, national security strategies of the new world order have shown continuity and evolution. This chapter's conclusions coincide with another study that found that "with the demise of the Soviet Union and the simultaneous strengthening of suicidal terrorist groups, containment and mutual assured destruction have slowly lost their applicability, and as a result, the last two administrations have attempted to redefine the purposes and efficacy of American power."[68]

Late in the second decade after the fall of the Berlin Wall, no president has defined the post–Cold War subtext more clearly than President Clinton did with his NSS of engagement and enlargement. Clinton's NSS may prove nowhere near as definitive as Truman's containment order but neither does the situation demand such focus. Nevertheless, engagement and enlargement set the tone for an active interventionist period in US foreign policy. Some major conflicts emerged, but the growth area was low-intensity conflict and operations other than war. Through the 1990s, the context of disengagement was less often about disengaging after major combat operations and more often about disengaging from *non-combat* operations.

Across both subtexts, the Cold War and the new world order, certain general lessons regarding disengagement are evident. The first lesson is that the disengagement of military forces does not always fit national security objectives. As noted in chapter 3, such cases as Korea, Bosnia, and Iraq during the NFZ enforcement era, where maintaining the status quo ante will require continued US presence, do occur. Fine, if the force is structured to support it, but the post–Vietnam force structure has declined precipitously. Current professional, high-tech military cannot expand its personnel and weapons pools like it could in 1950 or 1967. The complexity and cost of weapons, coupled with much greater costs and wholly different demands of the all-volunteer force, make such spikes unimaginable. The vastly smaller force structure also makes it much more difficult to maintain a large forward presence while still maintaining capabilities to engage in major regional contingencies.

The second lesson from the Cold War is actually a truism: the United States (or any nation) can disengage anytime it chooses, if it is willing to suffer the consequences for its actions. One cannot overstate that such cut-and-run disengagement is the least desirable way to disengage and is usually the result of poor engagement decisions or unforeseen changes in the operational environment. While President Kennedy may have considered such a withdrawal without victory in Vietnam, this approach actually has been used by the United States only in military-operations-other-than-war cases when lost face and credibility were trumped by lost lives. Taking Dr. Kissinger's observation, made retrospective to Vietnam, President Reagan in Lebanon and President Clinton in Somalia declared victory based on already accomplished objectives. The effect on the nation was nowhere near as catastrophic as it was in Vietnam, and both Presidents Reagan and Clinton subsequently won second terms. While Lebanon and Somalia were not Vietnam, disengagement is always an option—and not always the worst.

The third lesson carried over from the Cold War: the force used affects disengagement. Lower-scale forms of engagement ease disengagement. Regarding simplicity, first is the nonmilitary or the covert military operations like those the Reagan administration used in Latin America. Second, naval presence remained a classic coercive tool, and escort/defensive missions like Operation Earnest Will in the Strait of Hormuz offer serious firepower with relatively little risk. Third is airpower, with its non-combat mobility and ISR—expandable to include punitive air and cruise missile strikes like Desert Fox and further to cover full-blown air campaigns, either alone—such as those in Bosnia and Kosovo— or integrated into a full-spectrum, combined-force, coalition conventional war like Desert Storm or Operation Iraqi Freedom. The greatest barriers to disengagement arise once ground troops are introduced, but if ground troops are not used, an enforceable settlement is required for disengagement to occur, as evidenced in the Balkans and Iraq. Obviously, a time and place exist in the spectrum of conflict where ground forces are essential. From a disengagement perspective, however, it is best to put US ground forces in harm's way only when necessary, such as in Desert Storm or Iraqi Freedom. When ground forces are used, achievable objectives, a clear end state, and a planned turnover to a UN force foster disengagement, as was seen in Haiti.

Fourth, though it seems trite, is that the easiest intervention from which to disengage forces is the one where forces were never engaged because there was no militarily achievable goal matched to the deployable force. The initial attempt to land in Haiti is the perfect example. When this is ignored, as in the second Lebanon MNF and the follow-on Somalia deployments, disengagement is likely to be the ugly affair discussed above as lesson 2.

Beyond the lessons regarding what the United States has tried, what has worked, and what has not, another overarching problem in these cases abounds. Nearly coincident with the end of the Cold War, Congress studied the national security apparatus and legislated a reorganization of the DOD. The Locher Report studied the need for change and found the PPBS to be the root of DOD's strategy ills. From Locher came the Goldwater-Nichols Act, which drove the requirement for formally published NSS reports. As post–Cold War national security strategies expanded, national military strategies followed. This expansion led to the explosion in humanitarian, peacekeeping, and nation-building interventions that defined the 1990s—all despite shrinking defense budgets without concomitant changes to other areas of the national security apparatus. Still, the greatest effect of the end of the Cold War was perhaps budgetary. The perceived *peace dividend* really marks the point of departure between national security and military strategies. Expanding roles while simultaneously shrinking budgets and manpower made no sense: "The U.S. military in the 1990s was therefore placed increasingly in a dangerous situation as it became clear that it was neither sized nor shaped adequately for the grand strategic tasks it was being called upon to fulfill."[69]

In conclusion, military disengagement after attainment of realistic military goals helps to attain other national security ends, provided the means exist for the other instruments of national power. To this end, the next chapter examines the national security apparatus for organizational barriers to the imperatives for disengagement presented above.

Notes

1. Baldwin, *U.S. Grand Strategy*, 3.
2. Gaddis. "Grand Strategy of Transformation," 53.
3. Baldwin, *U.S. Grand Strategy*, 20.
4. US Congress, *Goldwater-Nichols Act*.
5. US Congress, Senate Committee on Armed Services, "Defense Organization," 483–84.
6. Ibid., 494.

7. US Congress, *Goldwater-Nichols Act*.

8. Baldwin, *U.S. Grand Strategy*, 29.

9. Reagan, "National Security Strategy," 1.

10. Reagan, "National Security Strategy," 1988, 1.

11. Ibid., 20.

12. Baldwin, *U.S. Grand Strategy*, 39.

13. Bush, "National Security Strategy," 1.

14. Barry, "Toward a New Grand Strategy." The concept of hard power is not discussed by Barry, but he borrowed it from Nye's book, *Soft Power*.

15. Bush, "National Security Strategy," 1.

16. Rooms, *Beginning With the End in Mind*, 15.

17. Donnelly, Roth, and Baker, *Operation Just Cause*, 58.

18. Ibid., 59.

19. Thurman, in foreword to Donnelly, Roth, and Baker, *Operation Just Cause*, xi.

20. Fishel, *Fog of Peace*, 29. See also Rooms, *Beginning with the End in Mind*, 17.

21. Donnelly, Roth, and Baker, *Operation Just Cause*, 25.

22. Schultz, *Aftermath of War*, 16.

23. Goemans, *War and Punishment*, 40.

24. Reprinted in Fishel, *Liberation, Occupation and Rescue*, 12. See also Bame, *Exit Strategy*, 25.

25. Bame, *Exit Strategy*, 26.

26. Ibid., 27.

27. Ibid., 29; Fishel, *Fog of Peace*, 33–34; and Cohen, "Intervention in Somalia," in Goodman, *Diplomatic Record*, 61.

28. Patman, *U.N. Operation in Somalia*, 92.

29. United Nations Security Council, *Resolution 794*.

30. Hempstone, "Think Three Times," 30; see also Bame, *Exit Strategy*, 31.

31. Sommer, *Hope Restored?* 70–73.

32. Bame, *Exit Strategy*, 31–32. Testimony to the House Foreign Affairs Committee, 17 December 1992, 7.

33. Bame, *Exit Strategy*, 31–32.

34. Brune, *United States and Post–Cold War Interventions*, 28.

35. Barry, ed., "Toward a New Grand Strategy."

36. Slantchev, *National Security Strategy*, 9; Bame, *Exit Strategy*, 34–35; and Howe, "U.S.-U.N. Relations," 16–17.

37. Bame, *Exit Strategy*, 36.

38. Baldwin, *U.S. Grand Strategy*, 42.

39. Sousa, "Is There Anything New? 6.

40. Sammon, "Bush's 'Grand Strategy.' "

41. Sousa, "Is There Anything New?" 7.

42. This phrase is borrowed from the title in Tami Davis Biddle, *Rhetoric and Reality in Air Warfare: The Evolution of British and American Ideas about Strategic Bombing, 1914–1945* (Princeton, NJ: Princeton University Press, 2002).

43. Clinton, "National Security Strategy," 2000, 4.

44. Brinkley, "Face the Nation" interview transcript, 23 September 2003, quoted in Baldwin, *U.S. Grand Strategy*, 42–43.

45. Clinton, "National Security Strategy," 84.

46. Baldwin, *U.S. Grand Strategy*, 42.

47. Ibid., 43.

48. Boot, *Savage Wars*, 283.

49. Slantchev, *National Security Strategy*, 14.

50. Bame, *Exit Strategy*, 37–38.

51. Ibid., 39–40.

52. Ibid., 40–41.

53. *New York Times*, "Poor Choice in Kosovo."

54. Pollock, "Roads Not Taken," 438.

55. Ibid., 433.

56. Mueller, "Demise of Yugoslavia," 13.

57. Ibid.

58. Slantchev, *National Security Strategy*, 13–14.

59. Mandelbaum, "Perfect Failure," 5.

60. Slantchev, *National Security Strategy*, 15. The incidents, their dates, and the parties responsible include the World Trade Center (26 February 1993, Islamic terrorists, possibly linked to al-Qaeda), the Khobar Towers (25 June 1996, Hezbollah, possibly assisted by Iran and al-Qaeda), the US embassies (7 August 1998, al-Qaeda), and the USS *Cole* in Yemen (12 October 2000, al-Qaeda).

61. Gordon and Trainor, *Cobra II*, 5; and Bush, "Period of Consequences."

62. Barry, ed., "New Grand Strategy."

63. Krauthammer, "Bush Doctrine."

64. Bush, "National Security Strategy," 2002, iv.

65. Clinton, "National Security Strategy," 6; Bush, "National Security Strategy," 4.

66. Bush, "National Security Strategy," 1.

67. Ibid., iv.

68. Sousa, "Is There Anything New?" 2.

69. Kagan, *Finding the Target*, 159.

Chapter 5

Reframing Disengagement
Organizational Barriers

Dismissing all thought of our land and houses, we must vigilantly guard the sea and the city. No irritation that we may feel for the former must provoke us to a battle with the numerical superiority of the Peloponnesians. A victory would only be succeeded by another battle against the same superiority: a reverse involves the loss of our allies, the sources of our strength, who will not remain quiet a day after we become unable to march against them.

—Pericles, 432 BC

Strategy attempts to effectively employ given forces to achieve stated objectives. If there is any mismatch, it must be that the objectives are too great to be achieved by available forces.

—Defense Organization: The Need for Change
Senate Armed Services Committee Staff Report

The notion of framing something is to focus on a moment in time, a scene, or a set of ideas. It can involve deliberate use of psychological, and intellectual skills, on the one hand, or less conscious skills within a sense of perception. Framing is a set of skills employed to one degree or another by the politician, photographer, chef, advertising executive, historian, teacher, coach, artist, academic, author, and by ordinary people.

—Strategic Leadership and Decision Making
Industrial College of the Armed Forces Text

In all our military training . . . we invert the true order of thought—considering techniques first, tactics second, and strategy last.

—B. H. Liddell Hart

83

> *War aims phrased in sweeping ideological terms are seldom capable of achievement.*
>
> —Samuel P. Huntington
> *The Soldier and the State*

This study has defined a place for strategic military disengagement in the NSS and the NMS. Presidential doctrines and representative conflicts since the end of World War II provide examples of how and when to disengage military forces from the full spectrum of military operations. Evidence suggests some forces at work prevent decision makers from considering, or at least choosing, disengagement. Recognized flaws in the US national security apparatus, which ultimately led to the Goldwater-Nichols Act, are used to frame the issue of disengagement in organizational terms less obvious, but ultimately more enlightening, than those typical of bureaucratic reform panels and commissions. This chapter posits barriers to disengagement in the US national security apparatus to determine if such weaknesses prevent linking the NSS to the NMS.

Organizational Barriers—The Locher Report

The aforementioned Locher Report, which led to the Goldwater-Nichols Act, sprang from the explosive growth in defense budgets during the Reagan administration. Goldwater-Nichols symbolizes organizational politics, as Congress tends to focus on the high-emphasis issues of the day. In studying the DOD, the report traced the evolution of the US national security apparatus, which really came into its current form after World War II. The DOD, the SECDEF, the Central Intelligence Agency, the National Security Council, and the US Air Force, as independent services, came into being through the National Security Act of 1947 (NSA 1947). Locher's commission used the NSA 1947 as the organizational foundation for its study.[1]

The Locher Report affects strategic military disengagement through its analysis of the weaknesses in American nonnuclear strategy making. The report notes that the DOD plans at two distinct levels—for allocation of resources and for contingencies or capabilities.[2] Locher concluded America's ills in non-nuclear strategy making were rooted in eight key flaws in the national security apparatus:

1. Dominance of programming and budgeting
2. Lack of management discipline in the Office of the Secretary of Defense (OSD)[3]
3. Inability of the Joint Chiefs of Staff system to provide useful strategic planning advice and to formulate military strategy
4. Lack of consensus on coherent military strategy and related policies
5. Serious inadequacies in the strategic planning machinery
6. Weaknesses in the services' strategic planning traditions
7. Inadequate policy and planning guidance
8. Insufficient guidance from the NSC.[4]

The Locher Report was not exclusively an attack on the DOD. It also pointed to Congress as the prime source of strategic instability and noted that continual congressional changes to funding and priorities made solid planning almost impossible.[5] Critics at the time went further by questioning Congress' ability to judge itself fairly as the creator and a major player in the national security apparatus. These critics concluded that serious change through reorganizing the DOD was unlikely. To the critics, at least as important as organization were other political and cultural barriers Congress erects through its "traditional American qualities of optimism (there need not be another war), ad hoc pragmatism (long-range planning is an undemocratic narrowing of options by technocrats), and openness (the public has the 'right to know')."[6]

This chapter echoes the critics of Locher, who argue that the national security apparatus involves much more than the DOD and the military. In addition, inasmuch as Locher focused exclusively on the military component of national power, the commission's view was limited and myopic. Demonstrating its bureaucratic roots, the commission analyzed the DOD from a structural perspective only and thus overlooked significant causes of strategy-making weaknesses in the DOD. Using Bolman and Deal's four-frame model is a proven tool for explaining past events and for predicting future ones and thus should help shed light on barriers that prevent strategic military disengagement.

Conceptually, the easiest idea to grasp here is one's personal *frame of reference*—how one observes, interprets, and acts in the world.[7] An individual, or indeed an organization, uses frames of reference as windows on the world and lenses that bring events into sharper focus, but they are also filters.[8] Filtering is important to disengagement, because it suggests that disengagement of military force gets overlooked and ignored because of some individual or organizational barrier to considering disengagement as a viable and valuable option. When historian and author William McNeill asserted, "What people think is the most important factor in history," he alluded to the importance of framing.[9] This study borrows the four frames offered by Bolman and Deal in *Reframing Organizations*: structural, political, human resources, and symbolic.[10] The book also describes each frame and explains how Locher's eight findings about DOD strategy making fit within the frames. More importantly, the frames highlight significant considerations overlooked by Locher.

Structural Barriers

The Locher Report was dominated by structural analysis, and thus most flaws it found with strategy making were described in structural terms. As the study was largely about reorganization, this is logical. The structural frame developed from the scientific management principles espoused by Frederick W. Taylor and the work of sociologists like Max Weber.[11] Ironically, the DOD planning, programming, and budgeting system, brought in by SECDEF Robert S. McNamara and criticized by Locher as the root of poor strategy making, also sprang from scientific management. Organizational charts, roles, and missions and division of labor between services and agencies typify artifacts of the structural frame. In the context of disengagement, the single most critical structural barrier is between the military, represented by the DOD, and other government agencies associated with the other instruments of power.

Locher's first noted flaw, the dominance of programming and budgeting in the PPBS, reflects a structural flaw that resulted in resource managers driving strategy. This structure was a product of the business-culture, scientific-management mind-set of Secretary McNamara and his whiz kids. The report did not attack the PPBS directly, for an enormously complex bureaucracy like the DOD could not function without an orderly system.

Second, Locher found fault with the PPBS in the unintended consequences it brought to strategy making. In the report's second finding, it found fault with the perceived lack of management discipline in McNamara's legacy OSD structure. Such a highly structured system of reports, directives, and decision memoranda provided easily measurable metrics for job performance. Strategy, by comparison, is more esoteric and not as satisfying, as it does not offer clear metrics of accomplishment. Taken from the structural view therefore, strategy and thus, disengagement, are overlooked. With limited emphasis on strategy writ large, the odds were long indeed of getting deeper than the purely military emphasis on weapons to defeat the enemy on the battlefield.

Compounding the lack of management discipline, in the view of the Locher Commission, was the placement of the joint chiefs in the organizational structure. Third, the report blames poor integration of the JCS in the budget process for the JCS system's inability to provide useful strategic planning advice and to formulate military strategy. In effect, the JCS could not positively affect disengagement decisions in the NMS because service budget commitments were made before JCS guidance inputs could influence them.

Fourth, Locher's finding of a lack of consensus on coherent military strategy and related policies recognizes the structural complexity inherent in "the largest and most complex organization in the Free World."[12] Structurally, barriers to disengagement exist within the DOD and among the various services and agencies on the proper use of forces. External barriers exist as well, with other agencies that stand to gain from having a military presence, be it for security, enforcement, or to back up threats. To build and maintain a coherent strategy in such an enormous bureaucracy is extremely difficult. The complexity of the task grows exponentially as the NSS it supports grows more expansive.

The fifth finding, regarding inadequacies in the strategic-planning machinery, seems structural because of the *machinery* metaphor. In systems management terms, this finding is about *process flows* or the way tasks are executed through the organization. Enormous bureaucracies have difficulty with large processes. Structurally, there are many diverse players with whom to coordinate. A strategic decision, including disengagement, must coordinate through a number of agencies and gain some consensus to have a chance at being executed.

Weaknesses in the services' strategic-planning traditions, the sixth finding, highlighted the lack of institutional structures to support strategy making. The report noted that strategic thought, especially grand-strategic thought in the form of NSS, was the root of this weakness and a product of World War II. Up to 1945 the US military had not begun to think in grand-strategic terms, and after the war nuclear weapons policy defined strategic thought. Additionally, from a structural standpoint, the military shunned strategic thought for tactical- and operational-level studies in their professional military education programs.[13] Disengagement is completely overlooked, as it is inherently strategic.

Weaknesses seven and eight—one noted as a finding, the other an unsubstantiated observation—both point to inadequate policy and planning guidance from the OSD and the National Security Council, respectively. Collectively, these weaknesses highlight the critical importance of clear objectives and intent for the formulation of effective strategy. Lack of clear guidance from the president, the NSC, or the SECDEF force military commanders to judge for themselves what the military strategy should be. Such abdications of guidance responsibilities hold particular importance to disengagement for reasons that illustrate why it is helpful—and even necessary—to view Locher through political, human resources, and symbolic frames.

Political Barriers

Whereas the structural frame represents the explicit, ordered, and rational design of an organization, the political frame represents the implicit, informal, and machinations of office politics.[14] Developed by political scientists, this Machiavellian frame is in the arena in which competing interests fight for power and scarce resources. Most important decisions in organizations involve the allocation of scarce resources. Deciding who gets what causes conflict in organizations. Power is the most important resource.[15]

Not to be viewed negatively, the political frame merely represents the reality of bargaining, negotiation, compromise, and coercion as necessary parts of organizational life.[16] Separate military services and various government agencies illustrate these political polarities. Strategic leaders have the positional power to set agendas, co-opt the activities of others, form coalitions, network, negotiate, and bargain to achieve agreement on certain plans of action. Even when direct power is limited, leaders may use other forms of power, including public opinion and political influence, to fulfill their personal agendas—even when those agendas run contrary to what a larger organization's leaders desire.[17]

The political frame offers the better view of the dominance of programming and budgeting on disengagement. Top-line budget authority equates to power, so the DOD should strive to keep military forces engaged. High operations tempo and demonstrated shortcomings in weapons, equipment, and training make it easier to justify ever-increasing budgets. Likewise, this arrangement fosters service parochialism. Service chiefs control the purse strings for their services, and since the services compete for the DOD budget, they must demonstrate their relevance to every fight. This encourages the services and the DOD to sign up for open-ended missions not necessarily suited to military skill sets. The battle for money and power favors engagement and by definition erects a barrier to disengagement.

Specific to Locher's context, and considering the impetus of the congressional study, the second finding regarding a lack of management discipline in the OSD may be viewed as a political backlash against the free-spending Reagan administration, where the OSD was rarely forced to make tough budgetary decisions. The critical aspect involved the lack of attention or prioritization the OSD gave to strategy making. Political drivers were prevalent, and the SECDEF and the OSD staff were so consumed with programming and budgeting tasks that what time remained was dedicated to reacting to congressional actions. As a barrier to disengagement, undisciplined management reflected the lack of civilian attention to or appreciation for the importance of strategy. When strategy is not a priority to national leaders, clear guidance and objectives are unlikely to come down to military commanders. The secretary also may be less likely to provide effective top cover to prevent military forces from being subsumed within diplomatic, economic, or information missions.

The inability of the JCS system to formulate military strategy is also best understood in a political frame. The report noted that important policy and strategy documents the JCS produced were neither timely nor authoritative enough to truly affect policy.[18] The lack of political power, or *teeth,* prevented the joint chiefs, resident at and responsible for the strategic level of warfare, from effectively establishing national military strategy. Politically, the service chiefs in the JCS system at the time had the power and used that power to resolve conflicts in favor of parochial service interests. Before Locher and subsequently Goldwater-Nichols, the services effectively planned and fought independently. Each service endorsed service-centric war plans aimed at predominance. As evidenced by the everyone-must-play mentality of Grenada, this shortchanged disengagement by offering forces not necessarily optimized for the mission at hand. Despite President Eisenhower's observation in 1958 that "separate ground, sea, and air warfare is gone forever," parochial service cultures still think this way.[19]

What Locher missed in commenting on the structural implications of the lack of consensus in the DOD concerning coherent military strategy were the political contradictions inherent in the huge national security bureaucracy. Politically, barriers to disengagement arise in the bureaucracy, as it takes a myriad of approvals to endorse a disengagement strategy but only one disapproval to kill it. These barriers are also indicative of the noted inadequacies in the strategic planning machinery. Resource competition and protection of service/agency agendas can push organizations toward ambiguous objectives and mission priorities. The focus at the Pentagon level is so resource focused that strategy is seen only through the lens of the long-term fight for program funding. Such compromises contribute to the objectives-force mismatches that lead to unwise commitments of military forces and the associated difficulties in disengaging those forces.

The last two flaws Locher noted were political ones, also. In the event of inadequate planning and policy guidance from senior leaders, barriers to disengagement arise from two issues of power. The two both enhance and work against each other, depending on perspective. On one hand, the military values the relative flexibility and autonomy of command. Military commanders want to be given clear guidance on what to do but not how to do it. On the other hand, civilian leaders, especially politicians, often prefer to keep strategic guidance vague. This prevents micromanagement but also preserves wiggle room for the policy maker. Barriers arise when planning and policy guidance is vague and nebulous to provide commanders clear, achievable objectives. Resultant open-ended missions without clear end states make disengagement difficult.

The eighth and final finding, regarding insufficient guidance from the NSC, was related to the seventh and, if valid, is critical. The Locher Report did not validate this view, claiming it was beyond the scope of the commission's study.[20] As with the general lack of sufficient planning and policy guidance, the effect on strategy generally and disengagement specifically is political, not structural. NSC guidance is particularly significant, as the NSC has the unique ability to bridge the NSS and the NMS. The NSC has been neither stable in composition nor consistent in its role over the 54 years of its existence. This does not support long-term consistency in formulating strategy. It erects a barrier to disengagement by not providing a stable, consistent, and predictable *goalkeeper* for the formulation and implementation of grand strategy. More importantly, insufficient guidance from the NSC fosters all the dysfunctional organizational issues previously addressed. By not taking the time or making the effort to clearly validate or invalidate this final finding, Locher's commission might well have missed the biggest key to the problem it studied. The decision to engage and disengage military forces rests in the executive branch. When the executive branch, whether in the form of the NSC or other agents, abdicates its responsibility for centralized management of government agencies with national security roles, lower-level organizational tensions usually intercede.

In the post–World War II era, perhaps no incident better illustrates the dynamic of the political frame than the power play between Pres. Harry Truman and Gen Douglas MacArthur during the Korean War. In an interesting display of one individual's frame of reference regarding military culture and politics, MacArthur believed once war was undertaken, all elements of national power rested with the theater commander. In January 1951 MacArthur feuded with the joint chiefs and civilian leaders over the response to China's entry into the war. MacArthur thought not expanding the war to China was appeasement. Leaders in Washington, however, wanted only to hold on to Korea and await an acceptable cease-fire and believed that expanding the war into China could not be less helpful to that goal. Still, the "great tradition of independence for the theater commander forbade them from questioning his reports."[21]

As the Chinese drove US and UN forces back and it appeared they might have to evacuate the peninsula, MacArthur felt Washington's policies were "booby trapped" to place on his shoulders any blame for Korea. MacArthur therefore applied his own political power in a report to the JCS, stating that "under the extraordinary limitations and conditions imposed upon the command in Korea . . . its military position is untenable, but it can hold, if overriding political considerations so dictate, for any length of time up to its complete destruction."[22] In effect, this reversed the trap. Threatening Washington with the complete and useless destruction of the forces in his command, MacArthur ensured he would be blameless, whether Washington sent reinforcements to enlarge the war or evacuated the peninsula.[23]

Human-Resources Barriers

In the previous example, Truman dealt with his political problem with a human-resources solution—he fired MacArthur. The fundamental premise of the human-resources frame is that organizations are composed of individuals with needs, feelings, and prejudices. The key to organizations' effectiveness is to match their needs with the abilities, skills, and attitudes of their people.[24] When General MacArthur's needs, feelings, and attitudes got too far out of alignment with the goals of containment, he was removed. Barriers to disengagement resulting from this frame come from mismatches of personalities and skills to critical strategy-making jobs and the protection of personal power and ego. Again, MacArthur's view of the war and his role in it were mismatched with and created a barrier to the Truman administration's goal of disengagement.

The importance of the human-resources frame is illustrated by the difficulty President Kennedy had in changing the military's focus to counterinsurgency. Andrew F. Krepinevich notes that the members of Kennedy's special group, Counterinsurgency, included no real experts:

> It has been noted that the group's chairman, General Taylor, had his focus on the problems of limited war, not counterinsurgency. Robert Kennedy, the president's brother, was a member of the group primarily as JFK's watchdog. This notwithstanding, his knowledge of doctrinal and force structuring requirements was minuscule. . . . Roswell Gilpatric, representative for the Department of Defense . . . was an individual whose Air Force background was largely irrelevant to the problem at hand. Murrow, McCone, and Bundy represented agencies that would be needed if a counterinsurgent capability were to be developed; none, however, came near to being an expert in counterinsurgency. Army Gen. Lyman Lemnitzer, chairman of the JCS, was not enthusiastic regarding the administration's push on low-intensity warfare.[25]

The other key human-resources finding from the Locher Report focused on inadequacies in the strategic planning machinery. From a human-resources frame, this inadequacy lies in the military policy of regularly moving personnel; thus, expertise in particular jobs is fleeting, and continuity is difficult to maintain. Regarding disengagement, this is important because engagements tend to take on a momentum (or inertia) all their own, which takes time to overcome. Even the right person, with the right vision and at the right place, may not have sufficient time to reverse the momentum of an engagement.

Also important are the biases inherent in players brought up in the varied cultures within the national security apparatus. Locher reflects an even worse example in the finding regarding the lack of management discipline in the OSD, as McNamara's system tended to put technocrats in positions where they did not necessarily have expertise in government policy or military strategy making. In human-resources terms, the JCS system was unable to formulate military strategy because the Joint Staff was afforded too few people, those the services provided were unqualified, and they faced unrealistic tasks.

Symbolic (Cultural) Barriers

These varied cultures are the emphasis of the symbolic or cultural frame. For most people drawn to government and military bureaucracies, the symbolic frame is the most unconventional view of an organization. Because it is a difficult analytical frame for those who see the environment as organized, structured, rational, and linear, its barriers are perhaps the most difficult to recognize and overcome. It helps to explain events in a volatile, uncertain, complex, and ambiguous environment. This frame sees the world epitomized by symbols of ethnicity, tribalism, religion, or myth. These symbols, rituals, and protocols define the culture of organizations.[26] In the discussion of barriers to disengagement, nothing is more responsible for erecting barriers than culture.

The Locher Report finding on inadequacies in the strategic-planning machinery is the only one to have relevance in all three frames discussed so far: structural, political, and human resources. The key to this flaw, though, is cultural. Military culture values action and tends to center on tactical expertise. US Army culture, or as Krepinevich calls it, the *Army concept* of conventional conflict with high volumes of firepower, tends to drive doctrine. Tactics associated with this doctrine dominated operational art, which in turn dominated strategy. Thus, the insidious effect of the Army's World War II paradigm was that it inverted the normal process flow of strategy determining tactics to tactics determining strategy (fig. 2).[27]

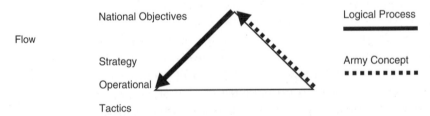

Figure 2. Effect of Army culture on strategy. Author's original conceptualization.

While all services share a bias toward tactics over strategy, to assume that the US military has a unified culture, however, would be a mistake. While NMS is inherently joint, it is not unitary. Joint culture does tend toward an Army bias. This causes problems, as Army culture is distinctly Clausewitzian, which is to say ground-centric. While Clausewitz gets an obvious pass on airpower, there is no excuse for his ignoring naval power. One could argue that disengagement is decidedly "un-Clausewitzian," as "in war the result is never final." However, if the NSS uses war as a means to pursue policy aimed at a continuing advantage, timely disengagement of military forces supports that end.

Overthrow and occupation are central to Clausewitz, and the Army, naval, and air cultures, generally, and US Navy and US Air Force cultures, specifically, are more open to disengagement, as their mediums are about control as opposed to conquest or occupation. Sir Julian Corbett, one contender as the naval Clausewitz, noted "the difference is fundamental."[28]

Despite the enormity of strategic planning, due to military culture, very few people and processes were dedicated to it. This is a critical barrier to disengagement, as military leaders tend to be much better trained, schooled, and experienced in the tactical skills and operational art of winning battles and much less so in the grand strategic realm where disengagement comes into play.

This very same cultural bias toward tactical versus strategic planning is the sixth noted flaw—the weakness of service strategic planning traditions. First, as noted in chapter 1, warfare did not become strategic in the way we think of it today until just within the last few centuries.[29] Locher characterizes US strategic thought as a product of World War II.[30] As the Cold War erupted in the aftermath of World War II, conventional strategy took a backseat to strategic nuclear policy. Individually and collectively, the American military culture always has celebrated individual acts of bravery, tactical prowess, and self-sacrifice. Service medals, battlefield promotions, and accolades like flying-ace status denote heroic individual acts. The warrior ethos is strong and critical to success on the battlefield. It is glamorous. Conversely, strategy is done in the rear. It is safe and boring. It is decidedly difficult, if not schizophrenic, to foster both a warrior ethos built on a can-do attitude of engaging and defeating the enemy throughout a career and then a strategic ethos that encourages saying no to missions and getting troops out of harm's way. *Nonetheless, disengagement is the ultimate purpose of military strategy. No one would plan a war or engagement to last forever.*

Locher's final two findings regarding guidance are primarily political. As discussed previously, though, their roots are at least cultural. American traditions of civil-military relations clearly affect disengagement. The strength of civilian control and the pervasiveness of civilian influence in military affairs change over time and within the context of particular conflicts. Since General MacArthur clearly struggled with a greater level of civilian influence than his previous experience in total, suggested global wars were warranted. Similarly, a whole generation of Vietnam-era generals felt hobbled by civilian meddling. The blowback from the *no more Vietnams* culture in the military eventually led to the Weinberger and Powell Doctrines, perhaps the strategic framework most conducive to disengagement—both by avoiding frivolous engagements and by mandating consideration of an exit strategy before engaging.

In sum, the Locher Report represents just one of many reviews of the national security apparatus since its inception in 1947. Its significance lies in its timing as an impetus for reform of the DOD under the Goldwater-Nichols Act. Viewing Locher's findings through the political, human-resources, and symbolic frames exposes several underlying factors that have dramatic effects on DOD strategy making that Locher's purely structural view overlooked. Thus, while Goldwater-Nichols is widely perceived as responsible for major improvements in the DOD's ability to conduct war at the operational and tactical levels, its effects on strategy making are less clear, echoing the critics of the time.

In spite of Locher and Goldwater-Nichols, and perhaps even because of them, several dangerous misperceptions persist that bolster barriers to disengagement. Even before the end of the Cold War, Locher was prescient on one hand, as it foresaw the need for change in the national security apparatus. By focusing so narrowly on the DOD, however, the report missed the mark. The National Security Act of 1947 is more of an anachronism today than it was in 1985.

Conclusion

This chapter explored the root of inappropriate congruencies between NMS and NSS. It examined potential organizational barriers to disengagement in the US national security apparatus. When the findings of the Locher Report are examined through four analytical frames, the central premise is found to be too simplistic. More than just fiscal tunnel vision, the *DOD's strategy-making ills were symptomatic of a poorly conceived national security apparatus.* Born of compromise in 1947 and allowed to stand too fundamentally unchanged, the system lacks the stability and enforcement of a unifying force. This allows clashes of culture, will, and power politics between the various agencies and departments to determine the direction of NMS. Such institutional anarchy leads to intervention decisions that ignore history's lessons for disengagement. Services vie for inclusion in all interventions for the sake of appearing relevant. Other agencies try to employ military forces for their own ends, and the military can be inclined to take on dubious missions to remain engaged and viable.

Notes

1. US Congress, "Defense Organization."
2. Ibid., 494.
3. The Office of the Secretary of Defense is often the victim of decidedly short-term congressional budgetary decisions that hinder strategic planning, but Locher points out that few in the OSD were experts in the financial processes they ran. Considering the political impetus of the congressional study, this may be viewed as political backlash against the free-spending Reagan era, where the OSD was rarely forced to make tough budgetary decisions.
4. United States Congress, "Defense Organization," 485; for the genesis of PPBS, see 498.
5. US Congress, "Defense Organization," 507.
6. Isenberg, "Missing the Point." This was a period of much focus on management processes. Business process reengineering was in vogue, as were the roots of what would become lean management, six-sigma, and other popular business-management trends.
7. Industrial College of the Armed Forces (ICAF), eds., *Strategic Leadership and Decision Making.*

8. Bolman and Deal, *Reframing Organizations*, 11.

9. McNeill, *Pursuit of Power*.

10. Bolman and Deal, *Reframing Organizations*, 15.

11. ICAF, *Strategic Leadership*.

12. US Congress, "Defense Organization," iv.

13. Ibid., 497.

14. ICAF, *Strategic Leadership*.

15. Bolman and Deal, *Reframing Organizations*, 186.

16. Ibid., 15.

17. ICAF, *Strategic Leadership*.

18. In theory, the Joint Long-Range Strategic Appraisal (JLRSA) and the Joint Strategic Planning Document (JSPD) should have been major cornerstones of military strategy. In practice, they were often just a "tortured synthesis of mutually contradictory positions" demanded by the services. See quote from Adm (Ret.) Elmo Zumwalt Jr., in United States Congress, "Defense Organization," 496.

19. US Congress, "Defense Organization," 49.

20. Ibid., 485; for genesis of the PPBS, see ibid., 498.

21. Millis, "Truman and MacArthur," in Guttmann, *Korea*, 72.

22. Ibid., 73.

23. Ibid., 74

24. Bolman and Deal, *Reframing Organizations*, 15.

25. Krepinevich, *Army and Vietnam*, 35.

26. ICAF, *Strategic Leadership*.

27. Osborn, in foreword to Krepinevich, *Army and Vietnam*, xi.

28. Corbett, *Some Principles of Maritime Strategy*, 94.

29. That is the way Sir Michael Howard would characterize it as in the late 18th century, roughly coinciding with the French Revolution, a convergence of large, standing, professional militaries serving national interests and capable of continual (vice seasonal) operations. See Howard, *War in European History*.

30. US Congress, "Defense Organization," 497.

Chapter 6

Effects of Barriers
Misperceptions and Overextension

1 May 2003 President George W. Bush stood on the deck of the aircraft carrier USS Abraham Lincoln, under a banner that declared "Mission Accomplished," and declared an end to major combat operations in Iraq.

—White House Press Release

The definition of victory is those two factors (changing the Hussein regime and finding and destroying Iraq's chemical and biological weapons . . . vice later focus on bringing democracy and freedom to the Iraqi people).

—Ari Fleischer
White House Press Secretary

None of us should be forever using military forces to do what civilian institutions should be doing.

—Condoleezza Rice, 2001
National Security Advisor

What is the role of the military beyond killing people and breaking things? Right now, the military in Iraq has been stuck with this baby. In Somalia, it was stuck with that baby. In Vietnam, it was stuck with that baby. And it is going to continue to be that way. We have to ask ourselves now if there is something the military needs to change into that involves its movement into this area of the political, economic, and information management. If those wearing suits cannot come in and solve the problem—i.e., cannot bring the resources, expertise, and organization—and the military is going to continue to get stuck with it, you have two choices. Either the civilian officials must develop the capabilities demanded of them and learn how to partner with other agencies to get the job done, or the military finally needs

99

*to change into something else beyond the breaking and
the killing.*

—Gen (Ret.) Anthony Zinni
Forum 2003

This chapter explores two macro-level results of the barriers
to disengagement that exist in the US national security apparatus. The chapter lays out common cultural misperceptions in
concepts and terminology that tend to make disengagement
difficult. It then posits several perceptions of strategy generally
and military force specifically that cause disengagement to be
seen negatively. These perceptions are key to America's traditional failure to plan for disengagement. By overcoming some
cultural (mis)perceptions, more parsimonious ends to conflicts
may be possible. Finally, the chapter shows how an overly optimistic, excessively ideological NSS can lead to an NMS that,
to maintain congruency, exceeds the capabilities, roles, and
missions of the armed forces as an element of national power.

Misperceptions Due to Organizational Barriers to Disengagement

The worst, most insidious effects of organizational and cultural barriers are the misperceptions they create, foster, and
exacerbate. In the broadest terms when applied to strategic
military disengagement, the DOD's organizational problems result in what international relations scholar Robert Jervis might
call elective attention.[1] By deferring strategy making to the services in favor of budget battles, the OSD ignores historical evidence that service culture is focused on winning on the battlefield. While this shade of victory reaffirms notions of US military
supremacy, it may prove hollow in light of poor focus on disengaging forces. The longer forces stay engaged without an achievable objective, the greater the chance the United States will fail
to achieve strategic victory, despite tactical battlefield victories.

National Power is Linear: Disengagement is Retreat

Misperceptions are rooted not only in organizational culture
but more broadly in national culture. One misperception of this

100

type that stands in the way of disengagement is the perception that national power is somehow linear, with war—or the use of military force—as being the end of a progression of options. Illustrative of this misperception is General MacArthur's testimony before the Senate Armed Services Committee and the Senate Foreign Relations Committee in early May 1951 as he answered a question about distinguishing military victory from political victory. MacArthur deemed them impossible to delineate.

> The ultimate process of politics; that when all other political means failed, you then go to force; and when you do that, the balance of control, the balance of concept, the main interest involved, the minute you reach the killing stage, is the control of the military. A theater commander, in any campaign, is not merely limited to the handling of his troops; he commands that whole area politically, economically, and militarily. You have got to trust at that stage of the game when politics fails, and the military takes over, you must trust the military, or otherwise you will have the system that the Soviet once employed of the political commissar, who would run the military as well as the politics of the country.[2]

MacArthur's statement simultaneously speaks to both parts of this misperception. First is the linear view that war is the end of a political continuum and somehow changes the normal rules for the use of national power. This view is not necessarily wrong or bad, but it is distinctly non-Clausewitzian. Viewed from either a Judeo-Christian or a liberal-democratic base, war as a last resort is morally and ethically sound. Indeed, it is reflected in the Weinberger and the Powell Doctrines' assertion that the United States should commit military forces only as a last resort. MacArthur's second point regarding who controls the elements of national power in war is arguably unconstitutional in the American system. Setting constitutionality aside, in American military culture, thinking of the military option as the end of a linear progression creates problems for disengagement. Ceding control of the instruments of national power to the theater commander biases national policy to the military's martial culture. Such abdication of civilian control over the military makes it difficult to see the disengagement of military forces and its concurrent return to diplomatic, economic, or informational instruments of power without reaching one of two conditions—victory or defeat.

Here, the military's negative, tactical connotation of the word *disengagement* causes problems. Like victory, disengagement is difficult to define at the strategic level. On the tactical battle-field, disengagement of forces without first achieving victory is a retreat. As discussed earlier, strategic victory is difficult to define except in total war. In limited war, and perhaps just as much in military operations other than war, disengaging military forces while the enemy still has the potential to resist is easy to construe as defeat. This is true not only for enemy propagandists but domestic situations, also. Politically, this is meaningful as domestic opposition to the president's administration can use disengagement as leverage.

No one personifies the negative political leverage of disengagement on policy better than Pres. Lyndon Johnson. Frederik Logevall argues that part of Johnson's decision not to disengage when the opportunity presented itself, but instead to commit combat troops to Vietnam, was rooted in his concern for personal credibility. His well-documented macho ethos left him unable to see disengagement as anything but "tucking tail and running."[3] Since victory at the strategic level is difficult, if not impossible, to define, it is imperative that military objectives, to include end state and disengagement, be clear and attainable. Otherwise, disengagement is easily portrayed as retreat.

The perception of disengagement as retreat is important for the image many Americans have of an "American way of war."[4] In this image, the United States protects and promotes its interests as a global power, and its actions always succeed. This image is also a fundamental part of US Army culture. America became a predominant world power after World War II, a decisive, total war ending in unconditional surrender for the Axis powers. This was the example of US foreign policy that stuck in the American psyche.[5] As alluded to earlier, Andrew Krepinevich asserts the Army concept of future war was further refined down to the period "from July 1944 to May 1945 in Western Europe." The Army, having made the necessary changes to adapt to that concept of future war, saw any situation that did not fit the mold as a special case, requiring no further long-term modifications to the concept. Korea and Vietnam were such special cases.[6]

Disengagement is anathema to this image. Reality differs from this image. National strategy rarely achieves its objectives in diplomacy, information, and economic realms, even if the military does. The difference occurs in cost. Failed diplomacy, sanctions, and propaganda efforts do not send body bags home to the United States, at least not directly or in large numbers. If there is an exception, odds are those bags are filled with military personnel. Therefore, while diplomats may still negotiate from untenable positions and sanctions can continue whether or not they have their desired effects, the military pays a tremendous price for leaving forces engaged without achievable objectives.

To dispel this misperception, note that disengagement does not even have to occur in a warring country. Taking troops out of allied countries can help relations as well. The George W. Bush administration did this in August 2003, removing US forces from Saudi Arabia. In this case the US presence was putting domestic pressure on the Saudi government and providing a target for terrorism. Disengaging military forces helped to maintain good relations and eased the way for other instruments of power to be more influential with an important ally, while destabilizing a pillar of support for Osama bin Laden and al-Qaeda.[7]

Victory Synonymous with Resolution—Disengagement Just Happens

B. H. Liddell Hart best sums up the problem with victory as follows:

> History shows that gaining military victory is not in itself equivalent to gaining the object of policy. But as most of the thinking about war has been done by men of the military profession there has been a very natural tendency to lose sight of the basic national object, and identify it with the military aim. In consequence, whenever war has broken out, policy has too often been governed by the military aim—and this has been regarded as an end in itself, instead of as merely a means to the end.[8]

Victory is hard to achieve in limited war partly due to limited commitment by the intervening state and insufficient stamina by the intervening state for protracted conflict.[9] There must be a plan, for disengagement does not just happen. In any intervention where the United States engages military forces with legitimate military objectives, there comes a time when those objectives are met. This defines tactical or operational victory.

If forces set objectives too low and leave too soon, they risk an incomplete victory by leaving a beaten, but not eliminated, foe. Conversely, if forces set the bar too high and wait too long to leave, they can lose domestic and international support, which strengthens the enemy's resolve.[10]

In popular media circles, it "has become fashionable to demand a linkage between the declaration of victory and the articulation of a specific and rapid exit strategy."[11] The popular notion of *exit strategy* as a euphemism for disengagement has tainted disengagement by association. Daniel Goure, senior defense analyst and vice president of the Lexington Institute, finds it fundamentally flawed to talk about exit strategies rather than military objectives and winning the war.[12] Likewise, former Speaker of the House Newt Gingrich testified to Congress that one of his "strongest messages in the Pentagon has been forget exit strategies. They don't exist. They're nonsense. They're not going to happen."[13]

The reality of disengagement, however, is that it must be driven by the achievement of military objectives in support of national strategy. As part of the culture of the so-called American way of war, in limited wars, after the United States achieves military victory on the battlefield, the cultural reflex is to consider the war over. The reality, however, is that, most US casualties (roughly 30,000 of around 33,000 total to date in Iraq) come in the post-conflict phase.[14] Limited wars bring a greater likelihood of residual violence after major combat operations. The trick is to accurately assess the point at which military forces have stopped being a force for suppression of violence and have instead become a target for violence themselves. Either way, disengagement rarely will be quick, and depending on the national objectives, it may not come at all. Regardless, it cannot be penciled in on the calendar before the objectives are accomplished. *Disengagement is a choice.*

Major Combat Operations Require Post-Combat Operations

Another misperception that goes against disengagement is the notion that major combat operations must, by definition, be followed by post-combat operations (PCO), also known as stability and security operations (SASO) and stability, security, transition, and reconstructions. In the English colonial period, Rudyard Kipling wrote of "The White Man's Burden." As secretary of state in the run-up to Operation Iraqi Freedom, Colin Powell allegedly warned of "the Pottery Barn Rule . . . a.k.a. you break it, you own it." This reasoning implies some paradox of power that the United States must be both bomber and benefactor. As with the pottery barn analogy, however, there is no such rule in national security. There may be several moral, ethical, and just plain good-neighborly reasons the United States does not want to go around the world killing people and breaking stuff without then going in and making things better for the innocent victims of interstate struggle. Yet, to make it a given is as imperially chauvinistic and condescending as Kipling's racist cultural satire. Still, pundits argue the manifest destiny of PCO and SASO daily.

Even Desert Storm, seemingly the poster child for correct disengagement—and in many ways the best example of US use of goals and limits in military operations—is a focus of this critique.[15] Nevertheless, Desert Storm is widely criticized for *not* falling victim to the above misperceptions. Desert Storm is a clear case of a decisive victory that created a successful postwar sanctions regime. It prevented the reestablishment of WMD programs, contained Saddam internationally, and left Iraq as a counterbalance to Iran for regional hegemony. Yet, some argue the United States ended the war prematurely, denied a stable postwar settlement, eschewed long-term political change, and "failed to bring about the demise of the vicious regime which had caused the problem in the first place, and it helped to trigger two civil wars and directly caused a breakdown in sanitation facilities in Iraq."[16] Other critics add the following:

> For all the effort President Bush and his advisors took in planning the liberation of Kuwait, they spent remarkably little time on ensuring a durable postwar settlement. In the period following the decision to announce a ceasefire [sic], the United States did little to translate its tremendous battlefield advantage into leverage at the bargaining table. Rather, it squandered its influence and in the process reduced its chances of achieving a lasting peace. Nobody in a position of authority in Washington or Riyadh had given much thought to how to end the war; almost everything had to be improvised.[17]

Some argue that "expecting military forces to redeploy rapidly upon the conclusion of decisive combat operations has little basis in history."[18] This is true. Even the successful execution of PCO in postwar Germany required a large military presence for more than four years. True again. When the United States occupies a nation after it has conducted major combat operations, conditions may require a large contingent of soldiers to support interagency personnel. But, this observation makes two false assumptions. First, occupation does not have to follow combat for the invasion strategy to effectively provide continuing advantage. Second, although it is likely in US interests to repair infrastructure and reestablish a functional society, this assumption does not then mean these acts become the US military's mission. These decisions are to be made according to the NSS. If the second assumption is desirable, it must be planned for and supported. Whoever is to take on the mission must be organized, trained, and equipped for the task. It cannot be an additional duty of the US military solely because its personnel are present.

The US Military Is the Only Organization That Can . . .

Related to the PCO misperception, but applied more generally, critics argue the US military should stop claiming peacekeeping and nation building are not its job. These critics claim the DOD should acknowledge that it is the only organization in the US government, and perhaps the world, that is capable of occupying and administering a nation until the host-nation government is reestablished and assumes control.[19] While this is fine to the point that it gets the military to think beyond the last bullet fired in anger, it does not mean it should be policy, for to do so would let the agencies that wield the non-military instruments of power abdicate their responsibility for any foreign policy failure involving the military.

Just because the United States or the US military is the only force in the world that can possibly do something does not mean it should be done. If the United States accepts that post-conflict operations and other operations other than war are necessary military missions, it must also accept that they are long-term missions. Tying up forces in non-combat missions

106

limits the ones available to react to emerging situations. Thus, accepting these roles requires changes to the US national security apparatus.

Worse yet is the more imperialistic extension of this misperception that the United States can do what the people of the target nation are unable or unwilling to do for themselves. To offer US military assistance or other assistance to a legitimate government for a cause for which its people are fighting is noble. To hope to affect change or impose a solution the people are not already engaged in, however, is folly. To modern Vietnam analogists, the situation in Iraq today reads like that in Vietnam in *the long 1964*. South Vietnam's political situation was dismal, and its leaders seemed unwilling to remedy the lethargy, corruption, and in-fighting in the government. Likewise, military leadership was corrupt, nepotistic, and cowardly. Desertion rates were high, and the public was war weary and at least leery of—if not outright opposed to—US presence. The lesson appears to be that the United States can help a country win a struggle, but it cannot win it for them. For the sake of disengagement, the implication of this misperception is that if the United States is the only country that can do something, then the United States will have to shepherd the issue over the long term.[20]

Overoptimistic NSS and Overextension

These barriers and misperceptions tend to lead the military into dubious missions. Particularly in the post–Cold War era, the military has been called upon in unpredictable ways and places. Jervis believes "the lack of major threats to vital American interests is an incredible boon to America and its allies, but it places unusual burdens on its military."[21] Employing military instruments for secondary national interests causes problems for the services. High operations tempo—including frequent training and extensive overseas deployments—are hard on the force, both for troop morale and equipment life-cycle sustainment. As fewer government civilians served in the military, they seem to have great difficulty in understanding why many non-combat activities pose serious problems for the military and fail to consult adequately on issues with a strong military component.

Overreach is not unique to the post–Cold War era. Korea is a classic case. Revisionist critics, including David Horowitz in the mid-1960s, viewed containment as exclusively a military doctrine, unsupportable by the other instruments of power. As such, it favored offensive action and could not be satisfied until it passed into liberation. In the Army's cultural view, as demonstrated by General MacArthur, the objective seeks the "elimination of the opponent, not a modus vivendi with him."[22] Horowitz finds the strategy of containment, as executed by MacArthur for President Truman, as the key determinant in the decision to *liberate* North Korea, the overreach that raised the stakes and extended the war. MacArthur's 1 October 1950 ultimatum for unconditional surrender ensured continuation of hostilities.[23] Following Horowitz's logic, strategic military disengagement is conceptually antithetical to containment, a concept based on regional and local balance of power.

Secretary of Defense Weinberger made structural arguments to resist US force deployments in the first Lebanon MNF in 1982. *Presence* was vague and nebulous and not a doctrinal mission for the US military. In fact, the *tests* Weinberger espoused, the so-called Weinberger Doctrine, are a perfect example of a structural barrier to engagement of US forces. Widely critiqued by both conservatives and liberals as being restrictive on the use of military forces, the Weinberger Doctrine nonetheless overcame the greatest barrier to disengagement by limiting the conditions under which US forces would be engaged in the first place.

The Lebanon case demonstrates how ill-conceived and ever-changing strategic objectives, especially when accompanied by an unclear military end state, erect political barriers to disengagement. The first MNF deployment featured a specific strategic objective that facilitated a similarly specific military end state: the PLO's evacuation from Lebanon. In contrast, the end state of the second MNF deployment was subject to changing strategic objectives and diplomatic actions. As the strategic objective changed, the military end state should have changed to conclude either with a well-planned withdrawal or an ambitious increase in offensive action.[24]

Instead, senior US officials tried to change their strategic objective while relying on a static military mission of *presence* and an ambiguous military end state of *stability*. Military planners could not address issues of transition to the diplomatic element of national power because that element, along with the strategic objective, continued to change. These ongoing changes also weakened the administration's public affairs strategy, since public pronouncements did not include a clear military end state or any evidence of progress toward strategic goals.[25] Political wrangling between agencies had resulted in military forces being engaged despite the protestations of the secretary of defense. *Once forces are committed, however, the political barrier leaves the DOD liable for failure to accomplish the mission.*

Crossing or restructuring traditional responsibilities can easily erect barriers to military disengagement by confusing roles and missions. Thus, when President Clinton's NSS declared the United States would "extend crime control efforts beyond [its] borders by intensifying activities of law enforcement and diplomatic personnel abroad to prevent criminal acts and prosecute select criminal acts committed abroad," it muddled military, law enforcement, and diplomatic roles.[26]

Overreach often begins with the misperception that only the United States can do something. This argument immediately becomes a barrier to disengagement when forces are employed. If the US military is the only organization capable of doing something and commits forces, how can the United States then disengage without clear victory? The United States was the only country that could keep the North Koreans from invading South Korea in 1953. This was true also as late as 1994. Why in 2007?

After the French lost its colonies in Indochina, only the United States could shore up the falling domino of Vietnam. Once in, it took more than a decade and a tightly woven web of rationalization to spin out without an outright defeat. The United States' successful disengagement from Lebanon's first MNF left it as the only country that could possibly operate the second MNF, though the force did not match the mission. Likewise in Somalia, UNOSOM II could not hope to match the original American mission, given smaller, less-capable forces and a more difficult and confrontational mission. So, America committed to give the mission its only hope for success. Finally, witness the Iraq northern and southern NFZs that followed a seemingly text-book disengagement of military forces and grew from subse-quent commitments of US forces to UN humanitarian and peacekeeping missions.

Similarly, the domestic argument is that only the military is manned and equipped for a mission, whether the mission is a military one or not. A common refrain in the current Iraq situa-tion regarding Phase IV stability operations and reconstruction is that the State Department and other civilian agencies are not manned and equipped to conduct such large-scale operations abroad. So, the military is left with questions like *If not us, then who*? In the interest of disengagement, when the tasks do not match the force, the answer to this question should be, *Not us . . . so*? Again, *the easiest way out of quicksand is to recognize it before stepping in.*

Political ideology is the strongest impetus to overreach. When ideological desires drive national security strategy, a great temptation emerges to apply military force to missions it is ill suited to carry out. Whether one considers President Clinton's peacekeeping and nation-building efforts to enlarge the com-munity of nations or Pres. George W. Bush's attempts to export Western-style liberal democracy, such lofty goals are mis-matched to the military's instrument of power and do not offer a satisfactory, militarily achievable end state.

Such efforts can be acceptable. In Korea, American desires for Cold War security trumped any other motivations. Disen-gagement was not a priority. Body bags stopped coming in after the 1953 armistice. The military was large enough to keep a contingent in Korea and valued presence around the world, particularly in the Sino-Soviet Eastern Hemisphere. As part of the Cold War paradigm, continued presence made sense. The ideological stand was capitalism versus communism. It did not matter that South Korea was not a real democracy until the 1980s. The ideological stand outweighed any perceived strate-gic gains from military disengagement. Likewise, the political realities of gaining French support for the postwar rearming of Germany and overall stability of Europe made backing and eventually replacing the French in Indochina seem worthwhile.

While the Korean model worked well enough for the situation in Korea, it did not prove viable against a Maoist insurgency in

Vietnam. Pres. Lyndon B. Johnson's National Security Memorandum 288 of March 1964 established a relatively benign American aim of "an independent, noncommunist South Vietnam" that could stand on its own.[27] Similar to Korea in its defensive posture and acceptance of a suboptimal indigenous government, the objective in Vietnam nonetheless proved militarily unattainable. The policy overreached, committing forces without achievable military objectives.

As chapter 3 showed, the American military often has faced disengagement dilemmas not resulting from major wars. Especially since the end of the Cold War, the United States has participated in numerous interventions to repair failed or failing states with infusions of liberal democratic principles. Such idealistic national strategic ends are difficult, if not impossible, to accomplish solely through military means. To succeed, it must be understood that all instruments of power have a role to play, and that role must be in harmony.

Even though the effort is well integrated, success is elusive when lofty ideological ends are in play. The best-planned example was the 1994 incursion into Haiti to restore Pres. Jean-Bertrande Aristide to power and finally to establish a functional democratic state. Despite extensive interagency coordination, good alignment of objectives to various agencies and forces, and a successful military disengagement and a turnover to the UNMIH, successes were short lived. Still, disengaging military forces and successfully transitioning to the UNMIH in March 1996 "allowed the U.S. to 'declare victory' without regard to UNMIH's eventual strategic success or failure in Haiti."[28] US leaders could attribute any future problems in Haiti to Aristide, UNMIH, or other factors. Defense secretary William Perry and JCS general John Shalikashvili dodged temptations to overreach through their consistent emphasis on meeting military objectives vice deadlines. [29]

Military disengagement worked in Haiti. Various common political barriers were successfully cleared to make this happen. First, troops were not engaged until their means were aligned with the desired ends. Other agencies' interests were not allowed to influence the commitment of forces. Once engaged, national security ends were kept realistic for the means available. It is tempting to overreach, especially in the face of success. Congress, other government agencies, the media, and service interests all are subject to this so called victory disease.[30] Yet, the record shows accomplishment of military goals facilitated diplomatic, economic, and information means. National security ends focused on realistic, continuing advantages to US and regional interests, vice idealistic Haitian interests. Much like the Reagan-era policy, even a minimally legitimate government was seen as favorable to more ambitious nation-building efforts.[31] Disengaging US forces and taking the United States face off the mission eased diplomats' return to primacy, provided victory for the information campaign, and strengthened the NSS.[32]

The easiest path to disengagement is to make smart decisions regarding when and how to intervene. Many cases fought after the Cold War, including some that were not really fought under the Cold War paradigm, seem to have erred by seeing military force as a shortcut to restoring stability or as a way to respond to a humanitarian crisis. This seems to imply, whether intended or not, that since the world's only remaining superpower can militarily defeat lesser states, there is no need to try other instruments of power.[33]

In the second Lebanon MNF and the NFZ operations in Iraq, the United States deployed forces to correct unforeseen strategic-policy failures following a successful, short-term military operation. US overreach in the second Lebanon MNF and the open-ended commitment to the Iraqi NFZ enforcement mission had dramatic long-term effects beyond those recognized at the time. The lack of finite, achievable mission objectives ironically gave the exit-strategy concept a bad name, as its discussion revolved around how and when US forces would leave unpopular interventions instead of how they would achieve a strategic goal.[34]

Expansive national security strategies encourage actions that require presence intervention. The military possesses the only pool of deployable personnel to provide that presence. Presence in non-permissive environments provides targets. The goals of peace operations too often have exceeded the resources put at their disposal. In terms of will, we often lack conviction in this area. Unless this changes, the United States must be more cautious in setting goals. Ideal objectives—like the maintenance of a multinational Bosnia—must not supplant practicable ones, like peaceful and fair secession.[35]

Imposing democracy is the classic example of overreach. It has almost always failed, including not only in Iraq in 2008 but also in every Clinton-era case. According to one study of peace-enforcement missions, "Nowhere have the liberal democratic military peacekeeping operations of the 1990s created liberal democratic societies. They did not even create much forward momentum in that direction, in any of the countries where they were deployed." The study found post–Cold War interventions under expansive national security strategies analogous to those at the end of the colonial era, where colonial powers struggled to leave positive influences behind. Disciplined militaries can establish order, but "liberal democratic states rarely demonstrate the will, or coherent policy direction, to transplant their values to other cultures."[36]

The Coalition Provisional Authority (CPA), set up to administer Iraq until an interim government could be elected, is a classic example of overreach. The national strategic objective in Iraq started out simple: to remove Saddam from power and to dismantle his WMD program. It evolved to the CPA mission of establishing "a durable peace for a unified and stable, democratic Iraq that provides effective and representative government for the Iraqi people, is underpinned by new and protected freedoms and a growing market economy; is able to defend itself but no longer a threat to its neighbors or international security."[37]

In sum, studying the relationship between national security strategies and national military strategies suggests the relevance of the KISS principle—keep it simple stupid. As the NSS has gotten more ideological, national military strategies have broadened, signing up the military to additional diverse missions. One study of national security strategies since Goldwater-Nichols found the current NSS to be built upon President Clinton's engagement and enlargement strategy, only tempered by Pres. G. W. Bush's sense of American exceptionalism. This so-called forceful engagement and enlargement promises a willingness to both threaten and use force to forward the goal of democratic enlargement.[38] So far, military force appears to represent a poor and insufficient means to this end.

Conclusion

This chapter explored the consequences of inappropriate congruencies between NMS and NSS. The analysis showed this *Lord-of-the-Flies* approach to national security also creates and fosters misperceptions about the limits of military power and its application, which further inhibit disengagement. Second, the chapter showed that overoptimistic, excessively ideological national security strategies can lead to national military strategies that, to maintain congruence, overextend the capabilities, roles, and missions of the armed forces as an element of national power.

As long as the current national security apparatus and its cultural image of the American way of war remain, disengagement lessons are likely to remain unheeded. This is found in the misperceptions wrought by the barriers to disengagement. Specifically, national power is not linear, particularly not when war is not total. Disengagement should not be equated with retreat. Likewise, military victory is not the same as strategic victory, and it neither signals the resolution of conflict nor initiates a timetable for disengagement. This is not to say that disengagement never can follow quickly on the heels of victory, but it cannot be assumed. Still, while post-conflict operations by military forces often will be required, it is also a misperception to believe this is always true. The argument that the military has to accept tasks because it is the only force capable of doing so is fallacious.

Robert Mandel mantains that "given the importance of proper disentangling from the arena of turmoil for not only military but also diplomatic and political ends, it is vital to establish early on a well-conceived exit strategy affecting the timing of military disengagement, but not allowing exit operations to become transparent or to be fully specified until stipulated victory conditions are achieved."[39] Disengaging before achieving valid military objectives designed to fulfill the national strategy can get troops out of harm's way, but that is not the primary point of disengagement. If strategic victory is accepted as being whatever the president or the NSC says it is, disengagement can occur quickly after accomplishing partial objectives. Departing too soon, though, can worsen the situation.

The incongruence of diplomatic and military cultures was clear in the conflicts of the 1980s and the 1990s. This incongruence defines the nature of the various instruments of national power. Diplomacy rests on cooperation and consultation to persuade. The military relies on force to coerce. Problems emerge when the two cross objectives. Thus, while *restoring stability* might work as a diplomatic objective, its vagueness allows for military disengagement. Military mission accomplishment needs to be defined in terms of defeating the enemy, then leaving when the job is done. Both Lebanon and Somalia demonstrated confusion between diplomats and military leaders over how each played into the national strategy. Desert Storm in Iraq and Haiti show how *diplomatic and military operations can work together when their objectives are clear and appropriate.*[40]

In setting national security strategy and establishing objectives, history suggests US policymakers should avoid setting the bar too high when proclaiming visions for postwar end states. The higher the bar is set, the harder it is to disengage. It is relatively easy to remove threats or restore order, given the proper force. Changing values and cultures takes longer, if it is possible at all. The same liberal democratic system the United States enjoys—and that seems so worth transplanting—also hinders the United States from conducting the long-term occupations necessary to make it stick. Furthermore, even when national will persists through extended reconstructions, the ultimate end state will likely be more a result of local realities than imposed structures. It is therefore better to aim for generic peace and stability, vice loftier goals, because "This leads to quicker withdrawals and fewer heartaches, even if the result will not be as ideologically tidy as exporting U.S. types of democratic institutions."[41]

Notes

1. Jervis, *Perception and Misperception in International Politics*, chap. 4.
2. MacArthur, "Testimony before the Senate Armed Services and Foreign Relations Committees," 38.
3. Logevall, *Choosing War*, 393.
4. Weigley, *American Way of War*, xx–xxii.
5. Bame, *Exit Strategy Myth*, 12.
6. Osborn, in foreword to Krepinevich, *Army and Vietnam*, xi–xii.

7. Hadar, *Sandstorm*, 72.

8. Liddel Hart, *Strategy*, 357.

9. Mandel, *Meaning of Military Victory*, 140; and Chye, "Victory in Low-Intensity Conflicts."

10. Mahnken, "Squandered Opportunity?" 125.

11. Mandel, *Meaning of Military Victory*, 164.

12. Beehner, *What Should Be the U.S. Exit Strategy from Iraq?*

13. Gingrich, Congressional testimony on way ahead for public diplomacy.

14. Collins, "Planning Lessons," 10. Casualty count was derived from Iraq Coalition Casualty Count Web site.

15. Terrill and Crane, *Precedents, Variables, and Options*, 46.

16. Mueller, "Perfect Enemy," 117, in Mandel, *Meaning of Military Victory*, 99.

17. Mahnken, "Squandered Opportunity?" 121, 136.

18. Rooms, *Beginning With the End*, 48.

19. Ibid., 10.

20. Logevall, *Choosing War*, xviii.

21. Jervis, "U.S. Grand Strategy."

22. Horowitz, "Containment into Liberation," in Guttmann, *Korea*, 230. Taken from *Free World Colossus* (Hill and Wang, 1965), 114–40.

23. Ibid.

24. Bame, *Exit Strategy Myth*, 23.

25. Ibid., 24.

26. Clinton, "National Security Strategy," 17.

27. Brower IV, "American Strategy," 8.

28. Bame, *Exit Strategy Myth*, 42.

29. Ibid., 43.

30. Mandel, *Meaning of Military Victory*, 79.

31. The so-called Kirkpatrick Doctrine, named for UN ambassador Jeanne Kirkpatrick, favored even unsavory authoritarian dictators over totalitarian communist regimes. This doctrine essentially follows a long tradition of "strange bedfellows" through US history. See interview, "Toward Humane Governance," *Religion & Liberty* (March/April 1992), available at http://www.acton.org/publicat/randl/interview.php?id=34.

32. Bame, *Exit Strategy Myth*, 44.

33. Ibid., 2.

34. Ibid., 3.

35. Conetta and Knight, "New US Military Strategy?"

36. Marten, *Enforcing the Peace: Learning from the Imperial Past*, 13–17.

37. Coalition Provisional Authority, *Vision for Iraq*.

38. Baldwin, *U.S. Grand Strategy*, 3.

39. Mandel, *Meaning of Military Victory*, 165.

40. Terrill and Crane, *Precedents, Variables, and Options*, 44–45.

41. Ibid., 11.

Chapter 7

Conclusion
Disengagement to Avoid Quagmires

The first notion the military strategist must discard is victory, for strategy is not about winning . . . war is but one aspect of social and political competition, an ongoing interaction that has no finality.

—Everett C. Dolman
Pure Strategy

The United States could and should disengage from the Middle East, since its presence there is not advancing U.S. interests; it is actually harming them.

—Leon Hadar
Sandstorm

If you concentrate exclusively on victory, with no thought for the after effect, you may be too exhausted to profit by the peace, while it is almost certain that the peace will be a bad one, containing the germs of another war.

—B. H. Liddell Hart
Strategy

If we don't have our security, we'll have no need for social programs.

—Ronald Reagan

Getting out of a war is still dicier than getting into one.

—Melvin Laird

Returning to the research question behind this study, the evidence suggests that too great a congruence between NSS and NMS negatively affects decisions on disengagement of military forces. Moreover, the relationship between the NSS and the NMS appears inverse; for as the NSS grows more expansive, the NMS needs to focus more on timely and efficient disengagement. Assuming a relatively small, professional, volunteer military force, an NMS of disengagement is the only way to ensure continuing advantage.

America needs to learn to disengage military forces from long-term deployments. The lessons of disengagement exist in theory and in history, but are often hard to grasp otherwise. Organizational barriers to disengagement exist at many levels. To help, disengagement needs to be defined, codified, and included in doctrine. Euphemisms of termination criteria, end state, and exit strategy are insufficient and create confusion.

Presidents decide when to use military force. They convey their philosophies of engagement of the military and other instruments of power through their national security strategies. National military strategy derives from the NSS and serves as the general guideline for using military force.

During the Cold War, the nuclear threat so dominated national security strategy that conventional relationships between the NSS and the NMS were fairly stable. The post–Cold War period has seen much more expansive national security strategies. In response, national military strategy has expanded to stay in step. Several factors have combined to dramatically increase the number and type of intervention missions taken on by the military.

Victory in such limited interventions is very difficult to define, but it is the metric the military culture expects to terminate operations and disengage. This tends to leave military forces in place after their militarily achievable objectives have been exhausted. Ultimately, victory is what US leaders define it to be through national objectives and desired end states. These must be kept realistic if the United States is to avoid quagmires.

In the current context, America usually will be seen as the best and most-qualified country to cure whatever ills exist. When the United States agrees to engage, it must remember the objective is to create a better state of peace. This does not mean the best state of peace conceivable. Weinberger and Powell were right. Military force should be used after other instruments of power have been exhausted. Also, their doctrine includes the continual reevaluation of the situation to determine the kind of conflict in which the nation is involved. This implies that if the context has changed beyond the point where US objectives are attainable, something has to change. The litmus test should be, "If we were not already engaged, would we enter this conflict?" More importantly, the Powell Doctrine is right in its implication that lives are saved by winning quickly and exiting in accordance with the strategy, vice going in with open-ended objectives or expanding the objectives in the wake of victory. In terms of lives, such thinking might well have saved the United States 80 percent of lives lost in Korea, greater than one-half of those lost in Vietnam, and virtually all of those lost in Iraq and Afghanistan.

When using force, the means used affect disengagement. Employing forces smartly does not conflict with the Weinberger/ Powell Doctrine assertion for overwhelming force. Naval forces offer worldwide, persistent presence with significant strike capability, while limiting exposure to irregular warfare forces. Similarly, air forces offer impressive physical and psychological presence advantages, with minimal exposure to threats. Most importantly, as the ground situation changes, air and naval engagements are both easily scalable. Ground forces pose the most difficult disengagement problems, so they should be used only when other means cannot be expected to achieve objectives.

Most questions concerning engagement versus disengagement are circular.[1] The more engaged we are, the more our interests get involved, and the more we feel compelled to act over every little thing. This is the history of engagement and enlargement as an NSS. Conversely, when we disengage, emerging problems no longer seem so pressing to us and the less inclined we are to engage.

Henry Kissinger is right. Objectives for interventions should be modest and attainable, preferably by US policy actions alone. Put another way, Occam's razor applies to national interests. The simplest, most parsimonious option is preferable. Staying to rebuild, PCOs, and SASOs in the hopes of spreading liberal democratic reforms may be a bridge too far.

At the root of all barriers to and misperceptions about disengagement lies the fact that *the US national security apparatus is broken.* Congress has studied it. Goldwater-Nichols attempted to fix at least parts within the DOD. In the end, though, reorganization can go only so far in fixing this problem. The structure, systems, and culture are all dysfunctional. If it is true that money is the root of all evil in Washington, then no one is more culpable than Congress. The only way to control intransigence among the varied agencies is to give the National Security Council budget authority. In 2008 agencies have separate funding streams, time lines, operational speeds, legislative requirements, agendas, personalities, and cultures. Congress could legislate a powerful NSC chief to marshal the various national security players toward sound strategy making, but to do so would surrender their own power of the purse to a more powerful executive branch office.

Disengagement does not imply animus toward any nation or region. Nor should it convey a desire to conserve resources. It is about US interests and preserving military force as a credible instrument of national power. Physical presence still may be required, but that presence should be as nonthreatening as possible. Strategic military disengagement helps to remove the *military face* from SSTR operations. This study recommends that other instruments of national power need to be built up to handle some of these missions but cautions that putting a civilian face on the force will not solve all problems. The colonial period was partly defined by many foreign *administrators*, so the perception of *imperialism* will not go away as combat boots are replaced by wingtips.

Military force exists primarily for making war, when necessary. The military instrument is otherwise limited as a strategic tool. Once committed, military forces quickly can become policy liabilities if not given proper objectives that are achievable by force. Once US forces are committed, history proves the nation has a vital interest in ending the conflict and disengaging military forces quickly. This is not to say as quickly as possible. The disengagement dilemma is that withdrawing forces too early is likely to breed future conflicts, while remaining engaged too long tends to forfeit battlefield victory. There is a balance between the resoluteness to see the mission through and the temptation to expand the mission in the shadow of military success. The best solution to the disengagement dilemma is to keep objectives simple and attainable, even if accomplishing the mission falls short of permanently solving all the issues. It may not be as satisfying as accepting an enemy's unconditional surrender, but in understanding the nature of the conflicts the nation enters, leaders must account for the possible end states consistent with that nature.

In closing, this study described the phenomenon of disengagement in the hopes of informing future decision makers. Still, in the end, without some prescription, the study only identified problems. Learning to disengage is not a lesson for the military or the DOD alone. The lesson is one of leadership, and thus resides at the top. Now is the time to learn the lessons, as strategic military disengagement is currently high on the national agenda. Only one prescription matters: the president and Congress must fix the national security apparatus. What Goldwater-Nichols started in the DOD must be expanded to encompass all instruments of national power. This is not the first study to suggest such action, and such a fundamental rethinking of national security is no mean feat. Yet, if serious action is not taken, beyond just reorganization, historical examples detailed in this and other studies should be kept nearby, because as a nation we will see them again.

Note

1. Ravenal, "Toward Disengagement and Adjustment," 45.

Bibliography

Allison, Graham T., and Philip Zelikow. *The Essence of Decision: Explaining the Cuban Missile Crisis.* New York: Addison-Wesley Educational Publishers, 1999.

Art, Robert J. *A Grand Strategy for America.* Ithaca, NY: Cornell University Press, 2003.

Bailey, Sydney D. *The Korean Crisis.* London: National Peace Council, 1950.

Baker, James A., III, and Lee H. Hamilton, cochairs. *The Iraq Study Group Final Report.* New York: Vintage Books, 2006.

Baldwin, Matthew. *In Search of U.S. Grand Strategy: National Security Strategy since Goldwater-Nichols.* Senior honors thesis, Duke University. http://www.poli.duke.edu/ugrad/2003%20honors%20theses/baldwinpaper.pdf (accessed 22 January 2007).

Bame, David J. *The Exit Strategy Myth and the End State Reality.* Quantico, VA: Marine Corps University, 2000.

Barry, Tom, ed. "Toward a New Grand Strategy for U.S. Foreign Policy." 13 December 2004 (updated 6 January 2005). http://www.irc-online.org/content/dialogue/2004/03.php.

Bassford, Christopher. "John Keegan and the Tradition of Trashing Clausewitz." *War and History* 1, no. 3 (November 1994). http://www.clausewitz.com/CWZHOME/Keegan/KEEGWHOL.htm.

Beehner, Lionel. *What Should Be the U.S. Exit Strategy from Iraq?* Council on Foreign Relations, 28 November 2005. http://www.cfr.org/publication/9288/what_should_be_the_us_exit_strategy_from_iraq.html.

Biddle, Tami Davis. *Rhetoric and Reality in Air Warfare: The Evolution of British and American Ideas About Strategic Bombing, 1914–1945.* Princeton, NJ: Princeton University Press, 2002.

Biden, Joseph R., Jr. "A Plan to Hold Iraq Together," *Washington Post,* 24 August 2006, A21. http://www.washingtonpost.com/wpdyn/content/article/2006/08/23/AR2006082301419.html?sub=new.

Bodenheimer, Thomas, and Robert Gould. *Rollback! : Right-wing Power in U.S. Foreign Policy.* Boston: South End Press, 1989.

http://www.thirdworldtraveler.com/Foreign_Policy/Global
RollbackNetwork.html.

Bolman, Lee G., and Terrence E. Deal. *Reframing Organizations: Artistry, Choice, and Leadership*. San Francisco, CA:
Jossey-Bass Publishers, 1991.

Bond, Brian. *The Pursuit of Victory from Napoleon to Saddam
Hussein*. New York: Oxford University Press, 1996.

Boot, Max. "The New American Way of War," *Foreign Affairs* 82
(July/August 2003).

————. *The Savage Wars of Peace: Small Wars and the Rise of
American Power*. New York: Basic Books, 2002.

Boule, John R., II. "Operational Planning and Conflict Termination." *Joint Forces Quarterly*, Autumn/Winter 2001–
2002, 97–102.

Brower, Charles F., IV. "American Strategy in the Vietnam War."
Lecture to Naval War College Senior Course, Newport, RI,
March 1992. In W. Andrew Terrill and Conrad C. Crane,
*Precedents, Variables, and Options in Planning a U.S. Mili-
tary Disengagement Strategy from Iraq*. Strategic Studies
Institute of the U.S. Army War College. http://www.strate
gicstudiesinstitute.army.mil/pubs/display.cfm?PubID=627
October 2005.

Brown, Seyom. "The Changing Circumstances of U.S. Foreign
Policy." In *The United States in World Affairs: Leadership,
Partnership, or Disengagement? Essays on Alternatives of
U.S. Foreign Policy*, edited by Robert A. Bauer. Charlottes-
ville, VA: University Press of Virginia, 1975.

————. "Korea and the Balance of Power." In Guttmann, *Korea: Cold War and Limited War*, 255. Taken from *The Faces
of Power: Constancy and Change in United States Foreign
Policy from Truman to Johnson*. New York: Columbia University Press, 1968.

Brune, Lester H. *The United States and Post–Cold War Interven-
tions*. Claremont, CA: Regina Books, 1998, 28. In *The Exit
Strategy Myth and the End State Reality*, edited by David J.
Bame. Quantico, VA: Marine Corps University, 2000.

Bush, George H. W. *The National Security Strategy of the United
States of America*, 1993.

Bush, George W. *The National Security Strategy of the United
States of America*. 2002.

———. "A Period of Consequences." Citadel, 23 September 1999. http://citadel.edu/r3/pao/addresses/pres_bush.html.

Carpenter, Ted Galen. "U.S. Aid to Anti-Communist Rebels: The 'Reagan Doctrine' and Its Pitfalls." *Cato Policy Analysis* 74, 24 June 1986. http://www.cato.org/pubs/pas/pa074.html.

Carter, Jimmy. *Presidential Directive/NSC-63: Persian Gulf Security Framework.* White House, 15 January 1981.

Chairman, Joint Chiefs of Staff. *The National Military Strategy of the United States of America: A Strategy for Today, A Vision for Tomorrow.* Washington, DC, 2004. http://www.dtic.mil/doctrine/jel/ other_pubs/nms_2004.pdf

Chye, Matthew Kee Yeow. "Victory in Low-Intensity Conflicts," 2000. http://www.mindef.gov.sg/safti/pointer/back/journals/2000/Vol26_4/4.htm.

Clausewitz, Carl von. *On War.* Edited and translated by Michael Howard and Peter Paret. New Jersey: Princeton University Press, 1989.

Clinton, William J. *A National Security Strategy of Engagement and Enlargement.* Office of the President of the United States. February 1996.

———. *The National Security Strategy of the United States of America,* 1998.

———. *The National Security Strategy of the United States of America,* 2000.

Coalition Provisional Authority. *Vision for Iraq.* 11 July 2003.

Cohen, Herman J. "Intervention in Somalia." In *The Diplomatic Record, 1992–1993,* edited by Allan E. Goodman. Boulder, CO: Westview Press, 1994.

Cole, Ronald H. *Operation Urgent Fury: The Planning and Execution of Joint Operations in Grenada, 12 October–2 November 1983.* Washington, DC: Joint History Office, Office of the Chairman of the Joint Chiefs of Staff, 1997.

Collins, Joseph J. "Planning Lessons from Afghanistan and Iraq." *Joint Forces Quarterly,* Issue 41, 2006.

Conetta, Carl, and Charles Knight. "A New US Military Strategy? Issues and Options." Cambridge, MA: Commonwealth Institute, Project on Defense Alternatives Briefing Memo No. 20, May 2001. http://www.comw.org/pda/0105bm20.html.

Corbett, Julian S. *Some Principles of Maritime Strategy.* Annapolis, MD: Naval Institute Press, 1988.

Cottrell, Alvin J., and James E. Dougherty. "The Lessons of Korea and the Power of Man." In *Korea: Cold War and Limited War*, edited by Allan Guttman. Lexington, MA: D. C. Heath and Company, 1972. Taken from *Orbis* 2 (Spring 1958): 39–60.

Crane, Conrad C., and Andrew W. Terrill. *Reconstructing Iraq: Insights, Challenges, and Missions for Military Forces in a Post–Conflict Scenario.* Carlisle, PA: Strategic Studies Institute, February 2003. http://www.carlisle.army.mil/ssi/pdffiles/ PUB182.pdf

Dicker, Paul F., Col, USAR. *Effectiveness of Stability Operations during the Initial Implementation of the Transition Phase for Operation Iraqi Freedom.* Center for Strategic Leadership, US Army War College, S04-02, July 2004.

Dictionary.com. *American Heritage® Dictionary of the English Language.* 4th Edition. Houghton Mifflin Company, 2004. http://dictionary.reference.com/browse/disengagement.

———. *WordNet® 2.1.* Princeton University. http://dictionary .reference.com/browse/disengagement.

Dillie, John. *Substitute for Victory.* Garden City, NY: Doubleday and Company, 1954.

Donnelly, Thomas, Margaret Roth, and Caleb Baker. *Operation Just Cause: The Storming of Panama.* New York: Lexington Books, 1991.

Dougan, Clark, and Stephen Weiss. *The Vietnam Experience: Nineteen Sixty-Eight.* Boston, MA: Boston Publishing Co., 1983.

Dower, John W. *Embracing Defeat: Japan in the Wake of World War II.* New York: W. W. Norton and Company, 1999.

Editorial. "A Poor Choice in Kosovo." *New York Times,* 24 December 2004.

Eliot, George Fielding. In introduction to Rutherford M. Poats, *Decision in Korea.* New York: McBride Company, 1954.

Fishel, John T. *The Fog of Peace: Planning and Executing the Restoration of Panama.* Carlisle Barracks, PA: Army War College Strategic Studies Institute, 15 April 1992.

———. *Liberation, Occupation, and Rescue.* Carlisle Barracks, PA: Army War College Strategic Studies Institute, 1992.

Frederiksen, Oliver J. *The American Military Occupation of Germany, 1945–1953*. Frankfurt, Germany: Historical Division, Headquarters, United States Army Europe, 1953.

Gaddis, John Lewis. "A Grand Strategy of Transformation." *Foreign Policy*. November/December 2003.

Galbraith, James K. "Exit Strategy: In 1963, JFK ordered a complete withdrawal from Vietnam." *Boston Review*, October/November 2003. http://bostonreview.net/BR28.5/galbraith.html#6.

Gelb, Leslie, and Richard K. Betts. *The Irony of Vietnam: The System Worked*. Washington, DC: Brookings Institution, 1978.

George, Alexander L. "American Policy Making." In *Korea: Cold War and Limited War*, edited by Allan Guttman. Lexington, MA: D. C. Heath and Company, 1972. Taken from *World Politics* 7 (January 1955): 209–32.

Gingrich, Newt. Congressional testimony on the way ahead for public diplomacy. Federal Document Clearinghouse Congressional Testimony, 11 June 2002. http://newt.org/backpage.asp?art=2235.

GlobalSecurity.org. "Operation Earnest Will." http://www.globalsecurity.org/military/ops/earnest_will.htm.

Goemans, H. E. *War and Punishment: The Causes of War Termination and the First World War*. Princeton: Princeton University Press, 2000.

Goodman, Allan E. *The Diplomatic Record, 1992–1993*. Boulder, CO: Westview Press, 1994.

Gordon, Michael R. " 'Catastrophic Success': Debate Lingering on Decision to Dissolve the Iraqi Military." *New York Times*, 21 October 2004, 1.

Gordon, Michael R., and Bernard E. Trainor. *Cobra II: The Inside Story of the Invasion and Occupation of Iraq*. New York: Pantheon Books, 2006.

Guttmann, Allen, ed. *Korea: Cold War and Limited War*. Lexington, MA: D. C. Heath and Company, 1972.

Hadar, Leon. *Sandstorm: Policy Failure in the Middle East*. New York: Palgrave Macmillan, 2005.

Hallenbeck, Ralph. *Military Force as an Instrument of U.S. Foreign Policy: Intervention in Lebanon, August 1982–February 1984*. Westport, CT: Praeger, 1991.

Hammel, Eric. *The Root: The Marines in Lebanon, 1982–84*. New York: Harcourt, Brace, Jovanovich, 1985.

Hankey, Lord Maurice. *Politics, Trials, and Errors*. Oxford: Pen-in-Hand, 1950.

Hanson, Victor Davis. *The Western Way of War: Infantry Battle in Classical Greece*. Berkeley, CA: University of California Press, 1989.

Hawkins, William R. "Imposing Peace: Total vs. Limited Wars, and the Need to Put Boots on the Ground." *Parameters* 30, no. 2 (Summer 2000). http://carlisle-www.army.mil/usawc/Parameters/00summer/hawkins.htm.

Hempstone, Smith. "Think Three Times before You Embrace the Somali Tarbaby," *U.S. News and World Report*, 14 December 1992, 30. In *The Exit Strategy Myth and the End State Reality*, edited by David J. Bame. Quantico, VA: Marine Corps University, 2000.

Hitchens, Christopher. "Powell Valediction." *Foreign Policy*, November/December 2004, 42.

Hobbs, Richard. *The Myth of Victory: What Is Victory in War?* Boulder, CO: Westview Press, 1979.

Horowitz, David. "Containment into Liberation." In *Korea: Cold War and Limited War*, edited by Allan Guttman. Lexington, MA: D. C. Heath and Company, 1972. Taken from *The Free World Colossus*. New York: Hill and Wang, 1965.

Howard, Michael. *War in European History*. Oxford: Oxford University Press, 1976.

Howe, Jonathan T. "U.S.-U.N. Relations in Dealing with Somalia." Paper delivered to Princeton University conference on "Learning from Operation Restore Hope: Somalia Revisited," April 1995, 16–17.

Huntington, Samuel P. *The Clash of Civilizations and the Remaking of World Order*. New York: Touchstone, 1996.

Ikenberry, G. John. *After Victory: Institutions, Strategic Restraint, and the Rebuilding of Order after Major Wars*. Princeton University Press, 2000.

Industrial College of the Armed Forces (ICAF), eds. *Strategic Leadership and Decision Making*. Washington, DC: National Defense University Press, 1999. http://www.ndu.edu/inss/books/Books%20-%201999/Strategic%20Leadership%20

and%20Decision-making%20-%20Feb%2099/pt1ch5
.html.

Isenberg, David. "Missing the Point: Why the Reforms of the Joint Chiefs of Staff Won't Improve U.S. Defense Policy." Cato Institute. Policy Analysis Number 100, 29 February 1988.

Jervis, Robert. *Perception and Misperception in International Politics.* Princeton, NJ: Princeton University Press, 1976.

Johnson, Dominic, and Dominic Tierney. *Failing to Win: Perceptions of Victory and Defeat in International Politics.* Cambridge, MA: Harvard University Press, forthcoming, chap. 1.

Joint Publication (JP) 1-02, *Department of Defense Dictionary of Military and Associated Terms.* Washington, DC: GPO, 12 April 2001, as amended through 1 March 2007.

———. JP 3-0, *Doctrine for Joint Operations.* Washington, DC: GPO, 10 September 2001.

———. JP 3-0, *Doctrine for Joint Operations.* Washington, DC: GPO, 17 September 2006.

———. JP 3-07, *Joint Doctrine for Military Operations Other Than War.* Washington, DC: GPO, 16 June 1995.

———. JP 3-07.3, *Joint Tactics, Techniques, and Procedures for Peace Operations.* Washington, DC: GPO, 12 February 1999.

———. JP 5-00, *Doctrine for Joint Planning Operations*, 2d Draft. Washington, DC: GPO, 10 December 2002.

Kagan, Frederick W. "War and Aftermath." *Policy Review* 120 (August and September 2003). http://www.policyreview .org/aug03/.

Karnow, Stanley. *Vietnam: A History.* New York: Viking Press, 1983.

Keegan, John. Introduction to Victor Davis Hanson. *The Western Way of War: Infantry Battle in Classical Greece.* Berkeley, CA: University of California Press, 1989.

Kennan, George F. *Russia, the Atom, and the West.* New York: Harper and Brothers, 1957.

Kennedy, John F. *Inaugural Address.* The Avalon Project at Yale Law School. http://www.yale.edu/lawweb/avalon/ presiden/inaug/kennedy.htm.

Kirkpatrick, Jeanne J. "U.S. National Security Strategy." Testimony to House Armed Services Committee. Washington, DC, 19 November 2003. http://www.aei.org/publications/ filter.all,pubID.19580/pub_detail.asp.

Kissinger, Henry. *Diplomacy*. New York: Simon and Schuster, 1994.

Koppel, Ted. "The USS *Vincennes*: Public War, Secret War." *Nightline* transcript. New York: ABC News, 1 July 1992.

Krauthammer, Charles. "The Bush Doctrine." *Time*, 5 March 2001.

Krepinevich, Andrew F. *The Army and Vietnam*. Baltimore, MD: Johns Hopkins University Press, 1986.

Laird, Melvin R. "Iraq: Learning the Lessons of Vietnam." *Foreign Affairs*, November/December 2005. http://www.foreign affairs.org/20051101faessay84604-p10/melvin-r-laird/iraq-learning-the-lessons-of-vietnam.html.

Liddell Hart, B. H. *Strategy*. 2d rev. ed. New York: Meridian, 1991.

Logevall, Frederik. *Choosing War: The Lost Chance for Peace and the Escalation of War in Vietnam*. Berkeley, CA: University of California Press, 1999.

MacArthur, Douglas. "Farewell Speech." West Point, NY: United States Military Academy, 12 May 1962. http://www.local voter.com/speech_dm1.asp. "Testimony before the Senate Armed Services and Foreign Relations Committees." In *Korea: Cold War and Limited War*, Lexington, MA: D. C. Heath and Company, 1972. Taken from US Senate. *The Military Situation in the Far East: Hearings before the Committee on Armed Services and the Committee on Foreign Relations*, 82d Cong., 1st Sess., 1951.

Mahnken, Thomas G. "A Squandered Opportunity? The Decision to End the Gulf War." In Andrew J. Bacevich and Ephraim Inbar, eds., *The Gulf War of 1991 Reconsidered*. Portland, OR: Frank Cass, 2003.

Mandel, Robert. *The Meaning of Military Victory*. Boulder, CO: Lynne Rienner Publishers, 2006.

Mandelbaum, Mandelbaum. "A Perfect Failure." *Foreign Affairs* 78 (September/October 1999): 5.

Marshall, A. *Phased Withdrawal, Conflict Resolution, and State Reconstruction*. Conflict Studies Research Centre, Central Asia Series. Swindon, UK: Defence Academy of the United Kingdom, 2006.

Marten, Kimberly Zisk. *Enforcing the Peace: Learning from the Imperial Past*. New York: Columbia University Press, 2004.

Martin, David C., and John Walcott. *Best Laid Plans*. New York: Harper and Row, 1988.

McGrath, Roger D. "The Western Way of War: From Plato to NATO." *Chronicles: A Magazine of American Culture*, February 2001, 13–15.

McNeill, William H. *Pursuit of Power: Technology, Armed Force, and Society since A.D. 1000*. Chicago: University of Chicago Press, 1982.

Millis, Walter. "Truman and MacArthur." In *Korea: Cold War and Limited War*, Lexington, MA: D. C. Heath and Company, 1972. Taken from *Arms and the State: Civil-Military Elements in National Policy*. New York: Twentieth Century Fund, 1958.

Mueller, Karl. "The Demise of Yugoslavia and the Destruction of Bosnia: Strategic Causes, Effects, and Responses." In *Deliberate Force: A Case Study in Effective Air Campaigning*, edited by Robert C. Owen. Maxwell AFB, AL: Air University Press, 2000.

———. "Perfect Enemy." In Mandel, *Meaning of Military Victory*.

Nye, Joseph S., Jr. *Soft Power: The Means to Success in World Politics*. New York: Public Affairs, 2004.

Oberdorfer, Don. *Tet!: The Turning Point of the Vietnam War*. Garden City, NY: Doubleday and Co, 1971.

Osborn, George K., III. In foreword to Krepinevich, *Army and Vietnam*, xi.

Patman, Robert G. *The U.N. Operation in Somalia*. Boulder, CO: Westview Press, 1995.

Peniston, Bradley. *No Higher Honor: Saving the USS* Samuel B. Roberts *in the Persian Gulf*. Annapolis, MD: Naval Institute Press, 2006.

Peterson, Steven W., Lt Col. *Central but Inadequate: The Application of Theory in Operation Iraqi Freedom*. Carlisle Barracks, PA: National War College, National Defense University, AY 2003/04 Course 5602, "The Nature of War." http://www.ndu.edu/library/n4/NWCAY04Index.html.

Poats, Rutherford M. *Decision in Korea*. New York: McBride Company, 1954.

Pollock, Robert D. "Roads Not Taken: Theoretical Approaches to Operation Deliberate Force." In *Deliberate Force: A Case*

Study in Effective Air Campaigning, edited by Robert C. Owen. Maxwell AFB, AL: Air University Press, 2000.

Posen, Barry R. *The Sources of Military Doctrine: France, Britain, and Germany between the World Wars*. Ithaca, NY: Cornell University Press, 1984.

Powell, Colin. *My American Journey*. New York: Random House, 1995.

Pribbenow, Merle L. *Victory in Vietnam: The Official History of the People's Army of Vietnam, 1954–1975*. Lawrence, KS: University of Kansas Press, 2002.

Ravenal, Earl C. "Toward Disengagement and Adjustment." In preface to *The United States in World Affairs: Leadership, Partnership, or Disengagement? Essays on Alternatives of U.S. Foreign Policy*, edited by Robert A. Bauer. Charlottesville, VA: University Press of Virginia, 1975.

Reagan, Ronald W. "National Security Strategy." 1988.

Record, Jeffrey. *Comparing Iraq and Vietnam*. Lecture presented to School of Advanced Air and Space Studies, Maxwell AFB, AL, 21 September 2006.

———. *Dark Victory: America's Second War against Iraq*. Annapolis, MD: Naval Institute Press, 2004.

Rooms, Travis E. *Beginning with the End in Mind: Post-Conflict Operations and Campaign Planning*. Fort Leavenworth, KS: United States Army School of Advanced Military Studies, United States Army Command and General Staff College, 2005.

Sammon, Bill. "Bush's 'Grand Strategy.'" *Washington Times*. 11 March 2004. http://goliath.ecnext.com/coms2/gi_0199 -129526/Bush-s-grand-strategy-Overlooked.html#abstract (accessed 19 March 2008).

Schultz, Richard H., Jr. *In the Aftermath of War: US Support for Reconstruction and Nation-Building in Panama Following Just Cause*. Maxwell AFB, AL: Air University Press, August 1993.

Slantchev, Branislav L. *National Security Strategy: New World Order, 1992–2000*. Department of Political Science, University of California–San Diego, 7 March 2005.

Smith, Martin. "Truth, War, and Consequences." *Frontline*. Public Broadcasting Service. Documentary aired 9 October 2004. Interview conducted 17 July 2003 with retired lieutenant general Jay Garner. http://www.pbs.org/wgbh/ pages/frontline/shows/truth/interviews/garner.html (Full transcript accessed 22 October 2004).

———. "Truth, War, and Consequences." *Frontline.* Public Broadcasting Service. Documentary aired 9 October 2004. Interview conducted 27 July 2003 with Kanan Makiya. 22 October 2004. http://www.pbs.org/wgbh/pages/front line/shows/truth/interviews/makiya.html.

———. "Truth, War, and Consequences." *Frontline.* Public Broadcasting Service. Documentary aired 9 October 2004. Interview conducted 5 September 2003 with Robert M. Perito, a career Foreign Service officer. http://www.pbs .org/wgbh/pages/frontline/shows/truth/interviews/ perito.html. (Full transcript accessed on 22 October 2004.)

Smith, Tony, and Larry Diamond. "Was Iraq a Fool's Errand?" *Foreign Affairs* 83, no. 6 (November/December 2004).

Sommer, John G. *Hope Restored?: Humanitarian Aid in Somalia, 1990–1994.* Washington, DC: Refugee Policy Group, 1994.

Sousa, Mariana. "Is There Anything New? A Comparison of Post–Cold War National Security Strategies." University of Notre Dame Political Science Department. Paper prepared for the International Studies Association Conference, 17–20 March 2004.

Speier, Hans. *Disengagement.* Santa Monica, CA: Rand Corporation, 1958.

Stanik, Joseph T. *El Dorado Canyon: Reagan's Undeclared War with Qaddafi.* Annapolis, MD: Naval Institute Press, 2003.

Strassler, Robert B., ed. *The Landmark Thucydides: A Comprehensive Guide to the Peloponnesian War.* New York: Touchstone, 1998.

Taw, Jennifer M. *Operation Just Cause: Lessons for Operations other than War.* Santa Monica, CA. RAND, 1996.

Terrill, W. Andrew, and Conrad C. Crane. *Precedents, Variables, and Options In Planning A U.S. Military Disengagement Strategy from Iraq.* Strategic Studies Institute of the U.S. Army War College. http://www.strategicstudiesinstitute. army.mil/pubs/display.cfm?PubID=627October 2005.

Thurman, Maxwell. In foreword to Thomas Donnelly, Margaret Roth, and Caleb Baker. *Operation Just Cause: The Storming of Panama.* New York: Lexington Books, 1991.

Turabian, Kate L. *A Manual for Writers of Term Papers, Theses, and Dissertations.* 6th ed. Chicago: University of Chicago Press, 1996.

United Nations. "General Assembly Resolution of October 7, 1950." In *Korea: Cold War and Limited War,* edited by Allan Guttman. Lexington, MA: D. C. Heath and Company, 1972.

United Nations Security Council. *Resolution 794 (1992).* 3 December 1992. http://daccessdds.un.org/doc/UNDOC/GEN/N92/772/11/PDF/N9277211.pdf.

US Congress. "Defense Organization: The Need for Change: Staff Report." Senate Committee on Armed Services. Washington, DC: Government Printing Office (GPO), 1985.

———. *Goldwater-Nichols Department of Defense Reorganization Act of 1986.* Washington, DC: GPO, 1986. Public Law 99–433.

———. *National Security Act of 1947,* 26 July 1947.

US Department of Defense. "Melvin R. Laird: January 22, 1969–January 29, 1973, 10th Secretary of Defense, Nixon Administration." http://www.defenselink.mil/specials/secdef_histories/bios/laird.htm.

———. *The National Defense Strategy of the United States of America.* Arlington, VA: Office of the Secretary of Defense. March 2005. http://www.comw.org/qdr/offdocs.html#nms.

US Department of State. "Statement by the President."

———. *United States Policy in the Korean Crisis: 1950.* Washington, DC: Division of Publications, 1950.

US Maritime Service Veterans. "Capture and Release of SS *Mayaguez* by Khmer Rouge Forces in May 1975." *American Merchant Marine at War,* 5 June 2000. http://www.usmm.org/mayaguez.html.

Weigley, Russell F. *The American Way of War.* Bloomington, IN: Indiana University Press, 1973.

Weinberger, Caspar. "The Uses of Military Power." Remarks prepared for delivery to the National Press Club, Washington, DC. 28 November 1984. http://www.pbs.org/wgbh/pages/frontline/shows/military/force/weinberger.html.

Winton, Hal. "An Ambivalent Partnership: US Army and Air Force Perspectives on Air-Ground Operations, 1973–1990." In Meilinger, *The Paths of Heaven*. Maxwell AFB, AL: Air University Press, 1997.

Wolk, Herman S. "The 'New' Look." *Air Force Magazine* 65, no. 8 (August 2003).

Worden, Mike. *Rise of the Fighter Generals: The Problem of Air Force Leadership, 1945–1982*. Maxwell AFB, AL: Air University Press, 1998.

Yost, David S. "The Future of U.S. Overseas Presence." *Joint Forces Quarterly*, Summer 1995.

Ziemke, Earl F. *The U.S. Army in the Occupation of Germany, 1944–1946*. Washington, DC: U.S. Army Center of Military History, 1975.

Zinni, Anthony. "Forum 2003: Understanding What Victory Is." United States Naval Institute *Proceedings* 129, October 2003.

After you have read this research report, please give us your
frank opinion on the contents. All comments—large or small,
complimentary or caustic—will be gratefully appreciated.
Mail them to the director, AFRI, 155 N. Twining St.,
Maxwell AFB, AL 36112-6026.

Learning to Leave

Brown

The Preeminence of Disengagement in US Military Strategy

Thank you for your assistance.